Ibsen and the Beginnings of
Anglo-Irish Drama

UPSALA IRISH STUDIES

In Cooperation with J. CARNEY, J. J. HOGAN, *and* N. G. HOLMER

Edited by

S. B. LILJEGREN

II

Ibsen and the Beginnings of Anglo-Irish Drama

I. John Millington Synge

By

JAN SETTERQUIST

Two Volumes in One

GORDIAN PRESS
NEW YORK
1974

Volume I Originally Published 1951
Volume II Originally Published 1960
Reprinted, Two Volumes in One, 1974

Published by Gordian Press, Inc.
By Arrangement With
Jan Setterquist
and
S. B. Liljegren

Library of Congress Cataloging in Publication Data

Setterquist, Jan.
  Ibsen and the beginnings of Anglo-Irish drama.

  Reprint of the 1951-1960 ed. published by Lundequist,
Upsala as vols. 2 and 5 of Upsala Irish studies.
  Includes bibliographies.
  CONTENTS: 1. John Millington Synge.--2. Edward
Martyn.
  1. English drama--Irish authors--History and
criticism. 2. Ibsen, Henrik, 1828-1906--Influence.
3. Synge, John Millington, 1871-1909. 4. Martyn,
Edward, 1859-1923. I. Title. II. Series: Upsala
Irish studies, 2 [etc.]
[PR8789.S4 1974]   822'.9'1209   73-22357

ISBN 0-87752-170-0

Contents

A close study of Ibsen in the course of many years made it clear to me, among other things, how difficult it was for contemporary dramatists to escape his influence. When attending Professor Liljegren's lectures on *English Literature after 1900*, I was induced to focus my interest on that part of his lectures which connected Ibsen with the early Anglo-Irish drama. I am grateful to him for suggesting the present subject as well as for help in many ways. I regard the essay now published as an instalment of a more comprehensive study which is actually in preparation.

J. S.

A NOTE ON IBSEN AND THE
IRISH LITERARY REVIVAL

There has always been an open enmity between the poet
and his critics as regards original inspiration. The poet wants
to be regarded as some sort of Minerva born complete and an
isolated genius out of a god's head. But the critic, who surveys
the field of literature, cannot fail to notice that the isolated
phenomenon is very rare if ever existent, and that at least this
field has a lot of parallels if he does not care to accuse the poet
of downright "thefts." The latter accusation was frequent
earlier, the critic could not see the difference between the
finished product of the genius and a poor model. Moliere did
not care to answer his critics and posterity has accepted him
because he was the genius who had a right to take his material
where he found it. An inimitable raconteur like Dumas hardly
keeps a rag of his literary output when his most eager critics
have finished unmaking him. But nowadays, the critic who e.g.
denies the genius of Tegnér in his admiration of Oelen-
schlager, cuts a poor figure. If not prejudiced, modern critics
are aware of the interdependence of all aspects of life, and we
all know how next to impossible it is to escape contagion or
influence in any part of human intercourse. It is not a question
of "theft" or loan any more, but a question of changing clay
into ore, so to speak, i.e. if handled by a genius. Otherwise,
clay will remain clay if not changed into something worse.

The interest in literary influences has been paramount in
criticism of our days. The purpose has been various. We

hinted above a case when a genius should be bereft of his national glory by means of would-be influence. But the purpose of the present study is different. Ibsen had the advantage of a hundred years accusation directed towards human society as in urgent need of reform, materially and morally. And he actually became the master mind who inquired into the inmost corner of conscience, and unveiled human frailty or even criminality. His genius overshadowed a period and is still more active than appears on the surface. The study of his impact on literature requires the mind of a scholar akin to the poet. To identify words is not enough, on the contrary, such an inquiry may lead astray.

Dr. Setterquist had all the advantage of an intimate absorption of the mind of Ibsen in his works, few studies could emulate him in this respect. And so he had the best starting point for two different tasks: the analysis of the mind of Synge in his dramas, and the analysis of Edward Martyn in his readings of Ibsen. Dr. Setterquist has achieved his task in an admirable way. He makes clear to us how Synge believed himself different from Ibsen when he changed the scene from middle-class respectability to longings, illusions, deceptions, superstitions, vainglory of beggars, vagabonds, and underlings in society. Synge believed himself free of the view of problems in human life pervading the work of Ibsen, but Dr. Setterquist proves the opposite fact. Synge's Nora has a problem as urgent as Ibsen's, and her resolution is identical. His study is as fine a tribute to Ibsen as to Synge.

From this essay with its delicate handling of sometimes hardly perceptible nuances of the mind or soul, we turn with equal expectations to Edward Martyn. *He* knew well enough that life was as full of problems as Ibsen had shown, and he tried to solve them as a conscious disciple of the great Norwegian. The study devoted to him is the more valuable because the author has a fine sympathy with the unselfish mind of Edward Martyn, ever ready to act subservient to great men and great movements, in his way more human though less gifted for drama than Synge. It would be devoutly to be wished for that Dr. Setterquist followed up these excellent essays in a comprehensive book on the subject, the more so as his scholarship has forgot practically nothing of pertinent material found in valuable investigations or unassuming articles.

S.B. Liljegren

Stockholm   1973

Introduction

Outlines of the Present Investigation

"Everywhere critics and writers, who wish for something better than the ordinary play of commerce, turn to Norway for an example and an inspiration."[1] Thus begins the famous manifesto which Edward Martyn, George Moore and William Butler Yeats published in 1889 in the first number of *Beltaine*, the official organ of the *Irish Literary Theatre*. They all thought highly of Ibsen and dreamt of doing for Ireland what he had done for Norway.[2]

Of the three Irishmen, Martyn was the one who most clearly revealed his dependence on the great Norwegian. Most of his plays show features found in Ibsen's later works. The resemblances are not slight or occasional but in every case there are fundamental similarities of subject-matter, character drawing and technique. It would, however, be premature to regard them as evidence of too close imitation. Martyn's work provides, among other things, an interesting example of how difficult, one might even say impossible, it was for the average dramatist of the period, enthralled by the skill of the Norwegian master, to preserve his originality.

The study of John Millington Synge, the dramatist who, with Yeats, was the principal representative of the early drama of the Irish renaissance, raises other, more complicated problems. In this connexion it may be of interest to quote the words of a German writer on Ibsen:

"Es muss — — — von vornherein gesagt werden, dass ein vollgültiger, apodiktischer Beweis nur in den allerseltensten Fällen möglich sein wird, eigentlich nur dann, wenn der betreffende Autor *selber*

---

[1] Ernest A. Boyd, *The Contemporary Drama of Ireland* (Dublin & London 1918), p. 8.

[2] Ernest A. Boyd, *Ireland's Literary Renaissance* (Dublin & London 1916), p. 291.

zugesteht, er sei von Ibsen beeinflusst. Denn selbst wenn einzelne Züge aus Ibsendramen in anderen Dramen englischer Autoren genau wiederzukehren scheinen, so bietet diese Tatsache immer noch keine absolute Gewähr für eine Beeinflussung, und auch der Beweis der Wahrscheinlichkeit bedarf meist noch anderer Stützen."[1]

The inquirer who wishes to trace the possible influence of Ibsen on Synge's dramatic output should begin by familiarizing himself with the opinions about Ibsen and the modern drama expressed by the Irish playwright on various occasions. Unfortunately, Synge's *Note-books* have not yet been published in their entirety. The material available at present therefore consists of the prefaces to *The Playboy of the Western World* and *The Tinker's Wedding*. The former introduction was written in January, 1907; the second in December that year. The preface to *The Playboy of the Western World* includes the following passage:

"In the modern literature of towns, however, richness is found only in sonnets, or prose poems, or in one or two elaborate books that are far away from the profound and common interests of life. One has, on one side, Mallarmé and Huysmans producing this literature; and on the other, Ibsen and Zola dealing with the reality of life in joyless and pallid words. On the stage one must have reality, and one must have joy; and that is why the intellectual modern drama has failed — — —"[2]

This short statement clearly reveals Synge's chief objection to Ibsen. He evidently finds the "joyless" Norwegian dramatist too depressing. Such an objection on the part of the author of *Riders to the Sea* is undoubtedly rather surprising. However, a similar opinion on Ibsen's problem plays appears in the slightly later preface to *The Tinker's Wedding* and shows Synge's attack on Ibsen to be not merely occasional and theoretical. Among other passages occurs the following:

"The drama is made serious—in the French sense of the word—not by the degree in which it is taken up with problems that are serious in themselves, but by the degree in which it gives the nourishment, not very easy to define, on which our imaginations live. — — —

[1] Robert Huber, *Ibsens Bedeutung für das englische Drama* (Diss., Marburg/L. 1914), p. 25.
[2] *Preface* to *The Playboy of the Western World* from *Two Plays* (Dublin 1911), pp. 4–5.

The drama, like the symphony, does not teach or prove anything. Analysts with their problems, and teachers with their systems, are soon as old-fashioned as the pharmacopœia of Galen—look at Ibsen and the Germans—but the best plays of Ben Jonson and Molière can no more go out of fashion than the blackberries on the hedges. Of the things which nourish the imagination humour is one of the most needful, and it is dangerous to limit or destroy it."[1]

Consequently, the Irish playwright in particular regrets the lack of poetry, joy and humour in the intellectual drama of Ibsen. Synge does not, however, intend to suggest that these qualities would of themselves impair or prevent the creation of problem drama. The tendency of his own plays bears ample witness to the truth of this statement. In fact, several Irish dramatists have shown that a typical Ibsen problem can be made to conform to the Irish sense of humour by means of a few trifling alterations. In this connexion it will be sufficient to mention the chief character of Rutherford Mayne's *The Drone* who has many features in common with Hjalmar Ekdal in *The Wild Duck*. But whereas, fundamentally, the latter is a tragic figure who awakens the sympathy of the audience, Daniel Murray in *The Drone* appeals primarily to its sense of humour. A similar change of attitude towards the problem is frequently adopted when Ibsen is transferred to an Irish milieu. Where Ibsen perceives a tragedy, his Irish fellow-dramatists often find the subject of a comedy.

What has been said of Rutherford Mayne is equally applicable to Synge. We may, on the whole, expect to find the same problems in his work as in Ibsen's, though he may formulate and develop them along the lines laid down in the prefaces to *The Playboy of the Western World* and *The Tinker's Wedding*.

We ought not, of course, expect to find literal borrowings from other authors in the work of a poet of Synge's standing. If we bear in mind the way of life usually portrayed by Synge, it is unlikely that we shall find any obvious resemblances between his figures and those of Ibsen. Our attention must therefore be concentrated on the manner in which both writers present their problems. In this way, we are likely to find out whether the Irish playwright

---

[1] *Preface* to *The Tinker's Wedding* from *Four Plays* (Dublin 1911), pp. 135–136.

has incorporated matter or manner from Ibsen's plays in this or that of his own dramas.

Our principal object, however, must be to ascertain to what extent the Ibsenian drama of ideas may have induced Synge to tackle the same problems and ultimately compelled him to find similar solutions. For Synge, in spite of his objection that "in these days the playhouse is too often stocked with the drugs of many seedy problems,"[1] is in a certain sense a writer of problem plays.[2] We have already uncovered the logical starting-point for such an investigation in the fact that Synge did actually read Ibsen and had adopted a very definite attitude towards him. The question, however, still remains—which of Ibsen's plays, or how many of them, did he read? There is, no doubt, a possibility that Synge familiarized himself with some of the plots of Ibsen's dramas merely by reading reviews of his plays. For all we know, he may even have seen Ibsen on the stage.

Synge's negative attitude towards Ibsen has of course increased the tendency to question *any* connexion between the two writers. William Archer, the well-known critic and translator of Ibsen, devotes an entire section of his book *The Old Drama and the New* to *The Coming of Ibsen* without even mentioning Synge's name. Indeed, he is almost too careful not to commit himself on this point as the following quotation shows: "If I were asked to lay my hand on a single English play which was obviously imitated from, or directly influenced by Ibsen, I should not know where to turn."[3] When we take into account, however, that Synge devoted his work to the description of one of Europe's most primitive communities, a complete contrast in every way to the milieu portrayed by Ibsen, we must, perhaps, not be surprised that the recluse of the Aran Islands should have escaped the notice of Archer.

On the other hand, it is most unadvisable to draw premature conclusions from the seemingly negative pronouncements of Synge on the subject of Ibsen. A Swedish critic very rightly points out how it often happens that a playwright announces, in a preface or an interview, that he has something to offer which is completely

---

[1] *Preface to The Tinker's Wedding.*

[2] See Chap. VIII.

[3] William Archer, *The Old Drama and the New* (London 1923), p. 307.

unlike Ibsen's drama. More often than not, the critic continues, the cleverly blended ingredients are identified as having been taken from the old master's pharmacopœia. The same authority goes on to say that the plays of Ibsen are the Rome of modern drama; all roads lead to it and radiate from it.[1]

Indeed the arrogant tone of Synge's attack is in itself an indirect proof of the fact that Ibsen occupied his thoughts more than he cared to admit, even to himself.[2] Although unwilling to anticipate the following investigation into the connexion between Ibsen and Synge, the present writer cannot at this point refrain from expressing the opinion that Synge's controversial attack was a form of self-defence. In other words, it is possible that Synge's artistic intuition gradually caused him to realize that he and the great Norwegian "poet of Problems" were in many ways kindred spirits. This supposition does not of course imply any derogation of or suspicious attitude towards the artistic programme launched by Synge simultaneously with his critical pronouncements on Ibsen. The point is, however, that we must not mistake the cause for the effect. An alternative which deserves consideration is offered by the fact that the positive part of Synge's artistic creed with its demand for "poetry," "joy" and "humour," may be interpreted as a conscious effort on Synge's part to free himself from the tyranny of the Norwegian dramatist. The history of the theatre includes more than one similar struggle, *e.g.* the Shakespeare—Marlowe case.

The question of literary influence involves an investigator in considerable difficulties. By pulling a single thread, he may disturb the equilibrium of the complicated network and thus incur the fateful danger of a one-sided point of view.

Despite the short duration of his life, Synge succeeded in acquiring a surprisingly comprehensive knowledge of both classical and contemporary literature. As a matter of fact, we know that he

---

[1] Martin Lamm, *Det moderna dramat* (Stockholm 1948), p. 87.

[2] One of Synge's friends, John Masefield, mentions Racine among Synge's literary favourites but with the following reservation: "I do not know who his masters in art may have been, that is one of the personal things he would not willingly have told." (John Masefield, *"John M. Synge"* in *Recent Prose*, London 1933, p. 203).

14

admired both the Elizabethan and the classical French drama. Among modern writers, other than Ibsen, who may have influenced him directly or indirectly, the following should especially be mentioned: Maeterlinck, Loti, Balzac, Hugo, Flaubert, Zola, Huysmans, Maupassant, France, Baudelaire, and Mallarmé. It will be noted that they are all French writers. The French influence on Synge's writing was accordingly noticed at an early stage.[1] However, the following critical objection on the part of a German authority clearly shows that its importance has been, at least to some extent, exaggerated. "Mag sein," he says, referring to the possible French influence upon Synge's dramatic inspiration. "Aber unter gemeinsamen Fabelboden fliessen die Formquellen in entgegengesetzter Richtung. Denn hier geht es irische Seelenwege."[2]

The aim of the present investigation is, not to question the originality of Synge, which of course precludes slavish imitation in any form, but to follow up a different trail which has hitherto escaped notice. As no account of the influence of the Ibsenian drama of ideas upon the writing of Synge has as yet appeared, it is conceivable that such a study may have a certain value also in order to modify all that has been said of Synge's indebtedness to French writers.

In an essay on reciprocity in literature T. S. Eliot says:

"Immature poets imitate; mature poets steal; bad poets deface what they take, and good poets make it into something better, or at least something different. The good poet welds his theft into a whole of feeling which is unique, utterly different from that from which it was torn; the bad poet throws it into something which has no cohesion. A good poet will usually borrow from authors remote in time, or alien in language, or diverse in interest."[3]

Even if, as occasionally happens, an author makes no secret of his literary models, for instance Bernard Shaw, James Joyce and Eugene O'Neill, to mention only some prominent Ibsenites of late,

---

[1] *e.g.* Maurice Bourgeois, *John Millington Synge and the Irish Theatre* (London 1913), Chap. IV and literature mentioned therein.
[2] B. Fehr, *Die Englische Literatur des 19. und 20. Jahrhunderts* (Berlin 1923), p. 503.
[3] T. S. Eliot, *Elizabethan Essays* (London 1942), p. 155.

it is an unusual procedure. It is also to be noted that such revelations are very often made at a time when the author in question has acquired an undisputed position in the world of letters.

However, it is much more usual for great writers, labouring under the impression of the completely erroneous idea that any kind of "borrowing" would impair their literary prestige, to go to the other extreme. With ill-advised zeal such authors categorically deny every foreign influence which might in any way cast a doubt on the original character of their own work. As is well known, Ibsen must definitely be regarded as a member of the latter group. One of the aims of the present investigation will be to find out whether and to what extent Synge must also be placed in this category.

CHAPTER I

In the Shadow of the Glen

A Doll's House
The Lady from the Sea

In the year 1903 Synge made his début with the one-act play *In the Shadow of the Glen*.[1] The play was performed under the most primitive conditions in a tiny makeshift "theatre." It was one of the first productions of the newly-constituted *Irish National Theatre Society*. The following year the same play was given by the members of the society at the recently founded Abbey Theatre.

*

The plot of *In the Shadow of the Glen* is a very plain one. The main theme is well known from many folktales: the old man who pretends to be dead in order to find out whether his wife is true to him. It may also be described thus; Synge depicts an unsuitable marriage between an old man and a young warm-blooded woman who has consented to the union solely in order to be provided for, and protected from the hazards of existence. The arrangement works well at first. But soon the man and his wife are involved in a kind of conjugal hide-and-seek. A shepherd who lives near by, begins to solicit the woman's favours. In that lonely valley it is of course impossible for the couple to keep the old man in the dark for long. He gradually begins to suspect that his wife is unfaithful to him in her mind and heart, perhaps even in deed.

In order to find out the truth, the husband puts up a sham death scene. Believed to be actually dead, he keeps very still under his

---

[1] This play is usually entitled *The Shadow of the Glen*. But in a note to the preface to *The Tinker's Wedding* it is called *In the Shadow of the Glen*. Consequently Synge's own name for it has been retained in the present study.

shroud and strains every nerve to watch the steps of his fickle wife. While she is keeping vigil by the "corpse" a tramp enters. She asks him to stay with the "corpse" while she fetches a neighbour to help her make arrangements for the funeral. As soon as he is alone with the tramp, the mock-dead man slowly rises from under his winding-sheet—and there is a farcical situation. However, the poor vagrant is soon won over and engaged in the old man's plot.

Later, when the wife comes back with her shepherd-admirer, the tramp becomes the witness of the scene when the furious husband drives her out of the house, threatening her and her partner with his stick. In this crisis the woman is deserted by the shepherd, who only cared for the money which he thought she would inherit from the old man.

But now the occasion is there for the tramp to play his part. In a poetical outburst of great rhytmic beauty he describes the wonder of a free vagabond's life, which captivates the woman's imagination. In the beginning she tries to ward off the seductive, inciting music of his voice, in fear of the hazards and anxieties the future may bring. But her horror of growing old and ugly at her husband's side overcomes her misgivings. She joins the tramp and departs with him to experience his life and the wonders of the dawn.

*

A critical scrutiny of Ibsen's works, taking as its starting-point the problem presented in *In the Shadow of the Glen*, reveals the fact that at least one of his "dramas of married life," *i.e. A Doll's House*, offers interesting points of resemblance to Synge's play.[1] *A Doll's House* was published in 1879 and the first English translation appeared as early as 1880.

The drama describes the marriage of two young people, the lawyer Torvald Helmer (later to become a bank-manager) and his

---

[1] Legouis & Cazamian, it is true, mention another of Ibsen's dramas in this connection: "Although the founders of the young Irish theatre are instinct with a spirit of reaction against the absolute sway which the Ibsenian model was wielding over the European stage, there is a suggestion of *Rosmersholm* in *The Shadow of the Glen*." (Legouis & Cazamian, *A History of English Literature*, London 1943, p. 1287.) This remark, however, leaves the impression as being somewhat hasty and ill-advised, and may the more readily be ignored, as no proofs are offered in support of it. (Cf. p. 20, note 1.)

wife Nora. Regarded from the outside their home appears to be a very happy one. Nora seems to lead a carefree existence as Helmer's lovely, spoilt plaything—his "doll-wife." When her husband comes home from his work, her only task is to amuse him and to satisfy all his whims. Because of her rapid movements Helmer calls her his "squirrel" or his "lark." She plays and sings and dances to amuse him, behaving exactly as her small children do when she romps and prattles with them. But according to Helmer that is just how the ideal wife should conduct herself. He takes no interest whatever in her thoughts or her opinions, reserving the right of a personal point-of-view for himself alone.

Living under these conditions, it is of course out of the question that Nora should be allowed to have any secrets from her husband. And so, when Helmer finds her surreptitiously nibbling sweets, he makes a scene. This storm in a tea-cup forms, as it were, something of an innocent prologue foreshadowing the great *scène à faire* in the last act of the drama. Here, Helmer loses all the illusions he has entertained about his clinging little doll-wife. Nora, on the other hand, stands changed from the mere plaything of her husband into a free and independent woman. Her belief in Helmer was founded on an illusion, namely, that he would be prepared to make as great a sacrifice for her sake, as she has shown herself to be capable of when her husband's health was at stake. And so the play ends with Nora preferring to leave Helmer and her children, rather than to stay and accept the humiliating conditions imposed on her by her husband.

*

The most obvious similarity of theme in the two plays is, of course, that both describe the difficulties caused by an unsuitable marriage. The outcome in Synge's play, as in Ibsen's, is that the woman leaves her home to face the hazards of the future.[1]

---

[1] Another amusing resemblance between the two plays, which appears to be more than a mere coincidence is that both heroines are called "Nora." Even if the name seems to be common enough in Ireland, there can be no doubt that Ibsen's play had caused it to be *à la mode*. It is significant that the first English translation of *A Doll's House* (1880) appeared under the title *Nora*. Cf. also Bernard Shaw's *John Bull's Other Island*.

As for the men, despite all the apparent differences between them, there is no doubt a certain likeness in their attitudes towards their wives. The complacent Helmer likes having a "doll" to play with. Synge's old man is equally contented with his lot, finding life peaceful and pleasant with someone to look after him and do the housekeeping in the lonely cottage. Neither husband allows his wife any kind of private life. The Norwegian Nora, like her Irish namesake, is spied upon by her husband, who suspiciously superintends all her actions. It is also worthy of notice, that both dramas conclude with the exposure of the heroine.

In both plays the final *scène à faire* ends with the victory of the woman who prefers to be the arbiter of her own destiny, turning her back upon the life of deceit and hypocrisy she can no longer endure. Synge's Nora, like Ibsen's, soon finds that her marriage has become a meaningless farce because her husband withholds his confidence from her and treats her as an inferior. Both Noras are women who have been so subjugated by their husbands that they feel like prisoners in their own homes. Each, therefore, suffers from unfulfilled, suppressed cravings. Synge's Nora, besides, is consumed by a kind of "horizon-fever," a secret longing for freedom which explains the attraction she feels for the tramp and the untrammelled beauty of the open-air life he leads. There is, of course, no trace of any such feelings in the Nora of *A Doll's House*.

But among the wealth of figures in Ibsen's famous gallery of women we find at least one who shares this mysterious longing for a dimly-perceived horizon—Ellida Wangel in *The Lady from the Sea*. This play appeared in 1888 and was shortly afterwards translated into English. Its influence was soon brought to bear on the Irish drama, notably in Edward Martyn's *An Enchanted Sea*.

Ellida Wangel, too, is living in an ill-assorted union, so that every circumstance of her life, even the view from her windows, seems calculated to encroach upon her individuality. As her husband, Dr. Wangel, says:

"Yes. There is this: that you cannot endure your surroundings here. The mountains oppress you and weigh upon your spirits. There is not light enough for you here—the horizon is not wide enough—the air is not strong and stimulating enough for you."[1]

[1] *The Lady from the Sea*, Act II. (*The Collected Works of Henrik Ibsen*, hereafter shortened "C. W.", vols. I—XI, London 1906–1908, IX, p. 223.)

Thus Ellida longs for the sea, to which she feels herself akin. Indeed, in the drama immediately preceding *The Lady from the Sea, i.e. Rosmersholm* (1886), Ibsen's portrayal of Rebekka West is clearly reminiscent of the heroine of *The Lady from the Sea.* For Rebekka, like Ellida Wangel, loves the sea. She is attracted by the wild coast of Finnmarken and feels imprisoned at Rosmersholm.[1]

Synge's Nora, too, has the same feeling of being buried alive "in the shadow of the glen." She gives vent to her dissatisfaction in the following pathetic outburst:

> "— — — what good is a bit of a farm with cows on it, and sheep on the back hills, when you do be sitting looking out from a door the like of that door, and seeing nothing but the mists rolling down the bog, and the mists again and they rolling up the bog, and hearing nothing but the wind crying out in the bits of broken trees were left from the great storm, and the streams roaring with the rain."[2]

Still another parallel between Ellida Wangel and Synge's Nora may be found in the fact that each is encouraged to break with her environment by a stranger who wishes to take her away from a world of shams and falsehoods. Ibsen's "Stranger," with whom Ellida has made a secret compact, a kind of half-betrothal, long before her marriage to Dr. Wangel, is analogous to "the Tramp" in *In the Shadow of the Glen.* In *The Lady from the Sea* the stranger says to Ellida Wangel:

"— — — I have come to take you away."[3]

The tramp besieges Nora and spurs her on with his enticing plea: "Come along with me now, lady of the house."[4]

---

[1] The theme, however, is not as all-pervading in *Rosmersholm* as in *The Lady from the Sea.* Nor does it as yet play so decisive a part as it is to do in the later play. Still it seems probable that this is the mutual theme which led Legouis & Cazamian, in a statement quoted above, to emphasize *Rosmersholm* and overlook *The Lady from the Sea.*

[2] *In the Shadow of the Glen,* p. 19. (The figures refer to the edition of Synge's plays mentioned in the introduction, of which *Four Plays* [Dublin 1911] includes *In the Shadow of the Glen, Riders to the Sea, The Well of the Saints* and *The Tinker's Wedding. Two Plays* [Dublin 1911] includes *The Playboy of the Western World* and *Deirdre of the Sorrows.*)

[3] *The Lady from the Sea,* Act III, p. 259.

[4] *In the Shadow of the Glen,* p. 27.

There is, however, another characteristic which "the Stranger" and "the Tramp" may be said to have in common. They are both symbolic figures. It is, indeed, most interesting to consider the two characters under that aspect. A Danish critic, who has made a comprehensive and penetrating study of Ibsen's dramas, points out the fact that it is a curious habit with Ibsen when one of his figures is drawn to another, to make the latter symbolic. Thus Brand is attracted by Gerd and the Ice Church; Ellida by the Stranger and the Sea; Solness by Hilde and Youth; Eyolf by the Rat Wife and Death.[1]

In the same mysterious way, Synge's Nora feels drawn to the tramp and all that he stands for, although she well knows that he may desert her at the next cross-road.

Who is he, then, this picturesque knight of the road who exerts such a strange influence upon Nora's mind and heart? Many critics have sought an answer to this question. The present writer regards the attempts made by some authorities[2] to deny the tramp any symbolic meaning whatever as an over-simplification of the problem. David H. Greene however, conducts his inquiry on other and more promising lines. "The tramp " he says "is not flesh and blood: he is a password to happiness."[3] That is certainly one way of putting it. One might however also be justified in following the postulate to its logical conclusion attempting the suggestion that the tramp symbolizes Life. Or, in simpler and more definite form, the life that has been crushed and stifled in Nora ever since she broke faith with herself and married the old man for purely material, egotistic reasons.

Ellida Wangel, too, has sold herself to her husband. She is, therefore, drawn in the same way towards the stranger and all that he represents; the sea and the life to which Ellida feels herself akin.

Thus, when the tramp comes to Nora, Life itself knocks at her door. Viewed from this angle, the tramp's last speech, filled with poetry, is Life's own call for Nora, a siren strain which removes every vestige of doubt and draws her unresistingly to him: "Come

---

[1] Henning Kehler, "*Studier i det ibsenske Drama,*" *Edda,* V (1916), p. 97.

[2] *e.g.* Maurice Bourgeois, *op. cit.,* p. 150.

[3] David H. Greene, "*The Shadow of the Glen and the Widow of Ephesus,*" *PMLA,* LXII (1947), p. 235.

along with me now, lady of the house — — — it's fine songs
you'll be hearing when the sun goes up — — —"[1]

As for the dramatic technique it is possible to find certain parallels between *In the Shadow of the Glen* and *A Doll's House*. In the
works of his mature period Ibsen shows a marked tendency towards
dramatic economy. The concentration he wishes to achieve is
attained by the deliberate avoidance, as far as it is possible, of
superfluous action. One result of the new method is that the dramas
become shorter and the characters fewer. There is a great contrast
between the three-act play *A Doll's House*, the cast of which com-
prises, strictly speaking, no more than five people, and its immediate
predecessor, *Pillars of Society*, which consists of four acts and has
nineteen parts.

In the works of Synge as in those of many other Irish playwrights
the art of dramatic concentration is frequently brought to the ut-
most peak of perfection. Even after he had made considerable cuts
in the first draft Ibsen required three acts to develop the theme of
A Doll's House. As a matter of fact, Synge succeeded in remodelling
the *motif* in the most severly-restricted of forms, that of the one-
act play.

Ibsen's daring break with the French tradition of the "happy
end" (usually "stuck on" to the play as an irrelevant afterthought),
"Scribe and Co.'s dramatic sweetmeats" as he contemptuously
summed up the whole genre,[2] excited much opposition at the time.[3]
Theatre-goers considered themselves entitled to be told what became of the characters in a drama. But the Darwinian theory of
Evolution had taught Ibsen that life never, or hardly ever, forms
a complete conclusion; it continues indefinitely. "The only possible
ending is death," says one of Ibsen's Danish friends, J. P. Jacobsen,
the first Scandinavian author to translate Darwin, "or else, since
human relationships are eternally inconclusive, one should finish
a work with an indication of further continuation, as Ibsen does
in *A Doll's House*."[4]

---

[1] *In the Shadow of the Glen*, p. 27.

[2] Theatre criticism of 13th April 1851, printed among *Artikler og Taler* in
the centenary edition of Ibsen's *Collected Works*, XV (Oslo 1930), p. 47.

[3] Ibsen's new technique was first introduced experimentally in *Love's Comedy* (1862), then more definitely in *A Doll's House*.

[4] Quoted from P. F. D. Tennant, *Ibsen's Dramatic Technique* (Cambridge

Some of Ibsen's later plays may also be said to end on a note of prophecy, *e.g. Ghosts* (1881) and *The Wild Duck* (1884), both of which close with a question-mark. The tendency to allow a drama to end on an uncertain note, so to speak, with a window open towards the future, is indeed so marked in Ibsen's work that we are obliged to assume that for him it was a matter of far greater importance than a mere technical subtlety. Indeed Ibsen himself had already expressed his general attitude towards his work in the often-quoted words:

"I prefer to ask, it is not my task to answer."[1]

The inconclusive ending is common to both *A Doll's House* and *In the Shadow of the Glen*. Ibsen's Nora, like Synge's, disappears into an obscure future. Both dramas end on a note of interrogation. If Synge had been asked, as Ibsen actually was, what became of Nora, he might well have agreed with his Norwegian colleague that he knew nothing about the future of the heroine. He had not even considered the matter, which he regarded as a side-issue.

*

In the above analysis the present writer has tried to draw attention to some of the chief points of resemblance in subject-matter, character drawing and technique between the play with which Synge made his dramatic début and Ibsen's *A Doll's House* and *The Lady from the Sea*. A few words must, however, also be said about the more striking differences in the two dramatists' treatment of the same subject.

The social position of Ibsen's chief characters and that of Synge's is a case in point. The action in both *A Doll's House* and *The Lady from the Sea* takes place in the milieu of the educated middle classes. To an outsider both these homes would appear safe and cosy, in the solid style of the 1880's. The contrast between the passionate life of his characters and the idyllic setting of the plays is, however, deliberately planned by Ibsen in order to heighten the effect, as he gradually unfolds his highly dramatic scenes.

1948), p. 117, as this author appears to have had access to material not printed in standard editions of J. P. Jacobsen's letters available in this country. The statement is made in a letter of March 14th, 1880.

[1] Ibsen in a rhymed letter to Georg Brandes in 1875. Cf. Synge's own statement: "The drama, like the symphony, does not teach or prove anything." (*Preface* to *The Tinker's Wedding*.)

24

In Synge's case, on the other hand, both theme and problem are given a simpler setting. Under these circumstances we cannot expect to find in the works of the Irish playwright any equivalent to the "bourgeois" atmosphere of Ibsen's dramas. Moreover, that milieu had already been exploited for artistic purposes, and Synge was determined to make an original contribution. He wished to obey the exhortation which Yeats, in his eager desire to place this strange youth in suitable surroundings, addressed to him in the following words:

"Give up Paris, you will never create anything by reading Racine, and Arthur Symons will always be a better critic of French literature. Go to the Aran Islands. Live there as if you were one of the people themselves; express a life that has never found expression."[1]

Although it is only natural that the creator of the Irish Peasant Drama should exclude from his works the middle-class background characteristic of Ibsen, we have already perceived in Synge's first play some typical Ibsenian problems, transferred to a lower and altogether more primitive level.

"The drama, like the symphony, does not teach or prove anything."[2] With these words Synge launches his anathema against the Ibsen drama. His reaction to the tendentious and moralizing "sermons" of Ibsen is violent. As a matter of fact the two dramatists differ markedly in this respect.

The didactic tendency, already noted in Ibsen's dramas of the 1860's, reaches its highwater mark during the 'seventies and at the beginning of the 'eighties. Referring to *A Doll's House*, it is certainly true that Ibsen, at a banquet given in his honour by "Norsk kvinde-sagsforening"[3] in 1898, publicly and categorically denied that he had ever consciously been a "feminist" author. But it should be noted that this statement was made towards the end of Ibsen's career, at a time when he considered himself justified in declaring that he had aimed at something much more important than the emancipation of women. In Ibsen's own words "the Cause of Humanity," not "the Cause of Women," appeared to the ageing

---
[1] W. B. Yeats, *Essays* (London 1924), p. 370.
[2] *Preface* to *The Tinker's Wedding*.
[3] A Norwegian association for the promotion of women's rights.

master to be the essential part of his message. This, of course, did not prevent him from giving every possible encouragement and support to the demands of the feminists as formulated in the endless discussions of the 1870's, when *A Doll's House* was conceived.

We have already found that Synge was opposed as a matter of principle to plays of the *Doll's House* type. However, the foregoing investigation has shown his keen interest in contemporary ideas and tendencies. The rapid and world-wide success won by Ibsen with *A Doll's House* must necessarily have made a strong impression on Synge. The detailed analysis of *In the Shadow of the Glen* has shown how skilfully he could evoke Ibsenian problems, re-arranging them to harmonize with his own interests and possibilities.

True to his artistic creed and as a deliberate protest against his prototype, Synge carefully refrains from allowing any of the characters in *In the Shadow of the Glen* to become a mouthpiece for the expression of personal opinions. The little one-act play has no tendency. Ibsen does not leave his heroine until the famous *scène à faire* between Nora and Helmer has made it possible for her to explain all her reasons for taking "the fatal step." How very different is Synge's method! He allows Nora to disappear with the tramp without even troubling to ask if what she is doing is right or wrong. The Irish dramatist, it should be noted, does not suffer from Ibsen's over-scrupulous conscience and predilection for the literary sermon. Where Ibsen would have raised a warning forefinger to "point the moral," saying "this is what happens when an old man takes a young woman for his bride," Synge simply states the facts with no moral reservations.

It seems therefore somewhat the irony of Fate that Synge's first play should immediately have forced him to become a martyr to one of his most important artistic principles—the idea of the "drama without a tendency." As a matter of fact, people considered the play to be an attack upon the Irish farmer's wife who had always been presented by the powerful Nationalist Party as a model of virtue in comparison with her British and Scottish sisters.

Incidentally, the plot of Synge's one-act play is based on a story told to Synge by an old Irish farmer and included in his book *The Aran Islands*. It is, however, amusing to note that the story in question is of a kind decidedly less pleasing to sensitive minds than Synge's own artistic adaptation.

The travel-sketches from Aran include many coarse narratives, which a dramatist of Synge's talent might easily have utilized in quite as effective a form as that of *In the Shadow of the Glen*. But, characteristically, Synge selected the story of the unsuitable marriage. In this, as in several of Synge's other works, there are many indications of his preference for literary themes which happened to be fashionable at the time.

The fact that the plot of *In the Shadow of the Glen* was of native origin does not in any way exclude the possibility that the immediate world-wide success of *A Doll's House* may have been an irresistible inducement to Synge to try his hand at the same problem.

In other words, Ibsen's drama might well have been the cause of the Irish dramatist's final decision to select that particular subject. In any case the work gives clear indication of being a variation of the well-known Norwegian theme.

CHAPTER II

Riders to the Sea

The Lady from the Sea
Rosmersholm

At about the time he wrote *In the Shadow of the Glen* Synge was writing another one-act play, *Riders to the Sea*, first performed in 1904.

The action of this play takes place on a small island off the west coast of Ireland. The plot is extremely plain and may be told in a few words.

*

The central figure of the drama is the old fisherman's widow, Maurya, the mother of six sons. Only the youngest, Bartley, is left to her. The sea has taken the others, as it took her husband. Bartley is now preparing to ride to the sea-shore on his way to a horse-fair on the mainland. The old woman, feeling the approach of disaster, tries in vain to persuade her son to stay at home. But Bartley refuses to be prevailed upon. He sets out, without his mother's blessing, on his red mare for the ride which Maurya with the audience is convinced will be his last. Shortly afterwards Bartley's sisters discover that they have completely forgotten to give him any food for the journey. Now his mother feels she must intercept her son and give him her bread and her blessing.

As soon as the old woman has gone, the two daughters begin to examine a bundle of clothes belonging to an islander who has been found drowned. At the opening of the play they had been looking at the clothes, but had hidden them from their mother, fearing they might have belonged to their lost brother, Michael. A further examination shows their worst fears to be justified. The sea has taken Michael as its prey.

At that moment Maurya returns, looking haggard and forlorn. She still carries the little parcel of food. Disregarding her daughters, she begins singing mournfully to herself. Asked if she has seen Bartley, she gives the evasive reply: "My heart's broken from this day." She then tells them that she has seen a most dreadful sight. Bartley was riding his red mare. After him came his grey pony. But its rider was now his brother Michael, dressed in his best clothes and with fine new shoes on his feet. The mother tried to speak, but could not utter a word. All of a sudden the frightful meaning of the vision was brought home to her. It was a portent. The sea was on the point of taking Bartley from her, too, as it had already taken her husband and her other sons. She remembers how under identical circumstances she lost her son Patch. She has scarcely finished telling her daughters of the tragedy, when several women enter the cottage. They make the sign of the cross and kneel down with their red skirts drawn over their heads as a sign of deep mourning. Maurya, feeling their presence rather than actually seeing them, asks dreamily if they are grieving for Patch or for Michael. She can no longer be kept in ignorance. They tell her that Michael has been found dead and laid to rest in the north of the island. The women have gathered in her house to wait for Bartley. His dead body is then brought into the cottage, wrapped in a bit of a sail which leaves a trail of sea-water on the floor. All, except Maurya, kneel at his bier, and the women begin to keen. But Maurya does not heed them. Her lifelong struggle with the forces of Nature has come to an end. She is beyond the reach of any earthly sorrow. "They are all gone now, and there isn't anything more the sea can do to me . . ." The old mother bends her head in resignation: "No man at all can be living for ever, and we must be satisfied." Thus ends this tragedy of a whole family beaten in their unequal struggle against the cruelty of an implacable sea.

*

As will be seen from the summary above, none of the characters in the play, not even the mother, has the central rôle in *Riders to the Sea*. For the sea itself, which Synge apparently regards as a symbol of Death, rules the lives of the islanders and controls their destinies. It is their sworn enemy; and yet also their perfidious ally.

For these people draw their sustenance from its depths. To the older generation who know the Atlantic in all its moods, and especially to the mothers, symbolized by old Maurya, it is the source of terror and woe and sleepless anxiety for those they love. But to the young people it is a lure and an enticement; its call makes them insensible to the warnings of their elders. Old Maurya sees with a heavy heart how her son leaves his home for certain death. "He's gone now, God spare us, and we'll not see him again. He's gone now, and when the black night is falling I'll have no son left me in the world."[1] The youthful confidence of her daughter offers an effective contrast to the old woman's complaint: "It's the life of a young man to be going on the sea, and who would listen to an old woman with one thing and she saying it over."[2]

Life—and death, that is the sea as reflected in the minds of two generations. The sea, which at the same time frightens and allures, repels and attracts its victims, is the very key-note of the play, and may be regarded as its catalyst. Unchangeable and invisible to the audience, the sea plays a fateful part in the drama, inexorably hastening the catastrophe which is foretold from the beginning.

If this introductory analysis of *Riders to the Sea* is placed as a basis for the scrutiny of Ibsen, it becomes obvious that his work during the 1880's includes two dramas which show several points of approach to that play. One of them attracts attention by its very title, namely *The Lady from the Sea* (1888). Because, in this drama, too, the sea may be said to play the principal part.

As has already been pointed out, the pivot of the plot is a discordant marriage. The wife, in her girlhood, was attracted to a man who like herself felt that he belonged to the sea, and she had never been able to muster up strength to rid herself of his influence.

In Ibsen's play, as in Synge's, the attraction of the sea is felt as a hidden undercurrent throughout the drama. Halvdan Koht, who is, perhaps, the greatest living authority on Ibsen, very rightly points out that in this drama the sea became both a spiritual power and a symbol. It represented, he adds, the attraction of the unknown—and, perhaps, of the primitive in man himself.[3]

---

[1] *Riders to the Sea*, p. 37.
[2] *Ibid.*, p. 37.
[3] Halvdan Koht, *Henrik Ibsen*, I–II (Oslo 1928–29), vol. II, p. 281.

Those who consciously deny the call of the sea, forfeit their peace of mind. Life on shore must of necessity seem incomplete to those whose affinities are with the sea. So it appears to Ibsen's heroine, Ellida Wangel. The fateful events of her youth have marked her for life. She is enthralled by "the Stranger" who symbolizes the sea, even in details such as the pearl of the pin, in his tie, as that pearl resembles the eye of a fish. As early as the first act, one of Ellida's girlhood friends gives vent to the following opinion about her: "I should rather say that you, Mrs. Wangel, stand in a peculiar relation to the sea and all that belongs to it." And Ellida answers: "Well, you may be right. I almost think so myself."[1] Her real feelings, however, are no doubt most clearly displayed in a long conversation with her husband, Dr. Wangel. "Night and day," she says, "winter and summer, it is upon me this haunting home-sickness for the sea."[2] When her husband in the kindness of his heart proposes to take Ellida out to "the salt-laden, sweeping sea-breezes" in order to cure her of her obsession, she cries out hysterically:

ELLIDA. Oh, don't speak of it! Don't think of such a thing! There is no help for me in that! I know, I feel, that I should not be able to throw it off out there either.
WANGEL. To throw what off, dear? What do you mean?
ELLIDA. I mean the terror of him. His unfathomable power over my soul—[3]

Towards the end of the drama there is a significant hint of the horror of the sea in the following dialogue:

WANGEL (*nearer*). Tell me, Ellida—what do you really mean by "terrible"?
ELLIDA (*reflects*). I call a thing terrible—when it both frightens and fascinates me.
WANGEL. Fascinates?
ELLIDA. Most of all when it fascinates me—I think.
WANGEL (*slowly*). You are akin to the sea.
ELLIDA. There is terror in that too.[4]

---

[1] *The Lady from the Sea*, Act I (C. W., IX, p. 187).
[2] *Ibid.*, Act II, p. 223.
[3] *Ibid.*, Act II, p. 235. (Lit. "I mean 'the terrible'; this incomprehensible power over the mind.")
[4] Lit. "So is the horror" ('the terrible'.)

WANGEL. And in yourself no less.[1] You both frighten and fascinate.[2]

The third act largely consists of a synthesis of Ellida's "philosophy of the sea"[3] and it ends with the following conversation, which offers a brilliant and comprehensive explanation of the lure "the Stranger" has for her:

ELLIDA (*softly and trembling*). Oh Wangel—save me from myself.
WANGEL (*looks anxiously at her*). Ellida! I feel it—there is something behind all this.
ELLIDA. All that allures is behind it.
WANGEL. All that allures—?
ELLIDA. That man is like the sea.[4]

In the *dénouement* of the last act Ellida succeeds in attaining spiritual freedom only after a terrible inner struggle:

ELLIDA (*with an outburst of emotion*). Oh—what is it that tempts and allures and seems to drag me into the unknown! The whole might of the sea is centred in this one thing![5]

Finally, when the transformation has taken place, Wangel says:

ELLIDA—your mind is like the sea: it has its ebb and flow.[6]

The sea and the attraction it exerts is not, however, the only element in *Riders to the Sea* reminiscent of Ibsen. As will appear from the above summary of the plot, there is a scene in which old Maurya tells her daughters of a vision she had. Her two sons, one of whom had already been drowned, appeared to her, astride their horses. The sight of the "Riders to the Sea" fills the old woman with horror. At once she knows for certain that she will never see her sons alive again. Shortly afterwards there is the news of Bartley's and Michael's fate. Of the former the narrative runs: "The

---

[1] Lit. "And the horror ('the terrible') in its turn is akin to you."
[2] *The Lady from the Sea*, Act IV, pp. 306–307.
[3] *Ibid.*, Act III, pp. 253–255 and *passim*.
[4] *Ibid.*, Act III, pp. 272–273.
[5] *Ibid.*, Act V, p. 341.
[6] *Ibid.*, Act V, p. 345. About 50 other allusions to the sea and its powerful influence upon man are to be found in *The Lady from the Sea*. As, however, they add little or nothing to the argument, the above quotations will suffice.

grey pony knocked him over into the sea, and he was washed out where there is a great surf on the white rocks."[1]

The suggestive vision of the horses and its interpretation as a portent of death is reminiscent of Ibsen's *Rosmersholm*, published in 1886. It so happens that there, too, visions, signs and portents play a considerable part. The "ghosts of the manor" are two horses which appear whenever someone of the family is going to die. Indeed this theme is so closely interwoven with the play that Ibsen originally intended to call it *White Horses* instead of *Rosmersholm*.[2]

The constant occurrence of symbols is a characteristic feature of Ibsen's work during the 1880's. They introduce an element of ambiguity into his plays during that period. With certain modifications this may also be said to be the case with Synge's first plays.

It has already been shown above that Synge uses the *motif* of the horses to presage the catastrophe. Likewise in *Rosmersholm* the heroine "in broad daylight" catches a glimpse of the white horses of the manor and feels them to be portents of impending doom.[3] "The white horses," Tennant says, "which haunt *Rosmersholm* help to give the suicide of Rosmer and Rebekka in the fatal mill-race an illusion of inevitability."[4] Thus they may also be said to exercise a certain influence upon the technique of the play.

Similarly, *Riders to the Sea*, is instinct with the same atmosphere of inevitability. This applies not only to the vision described above, but more particularly to the indomitable natural forces which are at work in the two plays. In both *Riders to the Sea* and *The Lady from the Sea* it has already been observed that an irresistible attraction is inherent in the sea. In *Rosmersholm* there is furthermore the mill-race which inexorably takes as its prey first one, then another member of the family, exactly as the sea does in *Riders to the Sea*. Koht is quite right in pointing out that there is one thing in particular in *Rosmersholm* that singles out this play from Ibsen's older works, *viz.* the power exerted by Nature over the human mind.[5]

---

[1] *Riders to the Sea*, p. 48.
[2] Koht, *op. cit.*, vol. II, p. 266.
[3] *Rosmersholm*, Act III (C. W., IX, p. 133).
[4] Tennant, *op. cit.*, p. 115.
[5] Koht, *op. cit.*, vol. II, p. 273.

The previous history of the characters in Ibsen's drama is as follows: The hero, Johannes Rosmer, is an idealist of the noblest type whose marriage is childless. His wife, however, although a noble woman, has not the mind best suited to helping him in his struggle to put into practice his utopian dreams of a community of noble souls. A young woman, Rebekka West, comes to Rosmersholm and by subtle suggestions she deliberately induces Rosmer's wife to believe that she is the real obstacle preventing her husband from fulfilling his mission. Finally Rebekka achieves her aim. Mrs. Rosmer, in a fit of desperation, throws herself into the mill-race and the new lady of the house takes her place as Rosmer's partner. Towards the end of the drama the master of Rosmersholm discovers that it was Rebekka, the woman he has ended by loving and trusting, who harried his wife to her death. And then he feels that he is no less guilty than she, and that only by voluntarily throwing themselves into the mill-race can they atone for their crime.

*

Thus the fatal mill-stream, which is never seen, but the roar of whose waters is heard in the distance throughout the play, gradually acquires the grandeur of a natural force which irresistibly sucks down the people of Rosmersholm, exactly as the sea does with the characters in *Riders to the Sea*.

Here, the objection may, of course, be raised that Synge might easily have found both the theme of the inexorable forces of Nature and the fatal vision of the horses in the storehouse of his island experience. As a matter of fact there is definite proof of his having done so in the latter case. Synge himself relates a little episode in his travel-sketches *The Aran Islands* which also seems to explain his choice of the rather peculiar title *Riders to the Sea*. The story, which is to be found at the end of the book, tells us how a young man was drowned on his way to the southernmost island. It is narrated in the following words:

"Before he went out on the sea that day his dog came up and sat beside him on the rocks, and began crying. When the horses were coming down to the slip an old woman saw her son, that was drowned a while ago, riding on one of them. She didn't say what she was after seeing, and this man caught the horse, he caught his own horse first, and then he caught this one, and after that he went out and was drowned."[1]

This, however, does not necessarily exclude a possible reminiscence of Ibsen. For the Aran book is full of such striking incidents which Synge, perhaps in part for lack of time—he began writing late and died comparatively young—but probably also for various other reasons, never put into use for a drama. Yet many of them would appear to be extremely suitable for dramatic purposes. It may suffice here to mention only the pathetic scene of a woman being evicted from her home: "The outrage to a tomb in China probably gives no greater shock to the Chinese than the outrage to a hearth in Inishmaan gives to the people," says Synge laconically.[2]

Here, as elsewhere, it may be presumed that the episode of the horses and, indeed, the whole of the evocative description of the sea, acquired additional dramatic significance for Synge when he saw the highly effective use to which Ibsen put similar themes in *Rosmersholm* and *The Lady from the Sea*.

The vision of the horses was, as has already been indicated, partly a technical device. It may, perhaps, be considered appropriate at this point to add a few remarks about the technique of *Riders to the Sea*.

Synge has been justly praised for his ability to evoke, with great economy of means, a vivid impression of the proximity and power of the sea. One of his biographers (Corkery) makes the following interesting observation:

"Synge makes the old woman, mother of many fishermen, never refer to the sea except as—the sea. Her phrases are: the sea; on the sea; in the sea; by the sea. There is never an adjective; no personification; no synonym. The word ocean does not occur. Yet how terribly aware of the malice of the sea we become!"[3]

On the whole, this passage could—*mutatis mutandis*—be applied to *The Lady from the Sea*. There is hardly a single qualifying ad-

---

[1] John Millington Synge, *The Aran Islands* (Dublin 1912), p. 222.

[2] Synge, *op. cit.*, p. 78.

[3] Daniel Corkery, *Synge and Anglo-Irish Literature* (Oxford 1947), pp. 140–141.

jective to be found in Ibsen's masterly hinting at the all-pervading
presence of the sea during the entire five acts of this play. Ellida
herself says simply "the sea," "on the sea," "in the sea," "over
the sea," "of the sea," "from the sea," and "to the sea."[1]

Furthermore, the sea is perceived from the stage in neither of the
two plays. Ibsen says definitely in one of his stage-directions:
"The open sea is not visible."[2] Primarily this may no doubt be
regarded as a concession to technical difficulties. On the other hand,
it is conceivable that both Ibsen and Synge were fully aware of the
fact that the mere mention of the sea and its power over man was
likely to make an even stronger impression on the audience than
if it were actually represented as part of the scenery. The same
calculation almost certainly accounts for the treatment of the mill-
race in *Rosmersholm*. The emotional effect of the fatal stream is
the greater because it remains invisible, the strange sound of its
rushing waters being only heard in the distance throughout the
action of the play.

The contrast between the small, dark cottage and the unseen
ocean outside it is quite in keeping with the "Ibsen tradition."
Indeed, it was a literary fashion for quite a long time to criticize
Ibsen for the stuffy atmosphere of his plays with their frequent
indoor settings. Somewhat premature conclusions as regards Ibsen's
attitude towards Nature were readily drawn from the fact that,
with the passing of the years, he became less and less inclined to
stir from his own hearth. But even a cursory reading of his stage-
instructions reveals the fact that, especially in his later works, he
was particularly fond of *outdoor* settings for his plays, such as a
mountainous or a coastal landscape.[3] And he retained his fondness
for the sea throughout his life. Even in this respect Ibsen's stage-
directions are, indeed, most illuminating.

In his delineation of "the Stranger," however, Ibsen used a
kind of "sea-symbolism" never found in the works of Synge. Here
it will suffice to recall Ellida's remark: "That man is like the sea."[4]

---

[1] *The Lady from the Sea, passim.*
[2] *Ibid.*, stage-direction for act II.
[3] See *e.g. Brand, Peer Gynt, The Lady from the Sea, Little Eyolf, John Gabriel Borkman*, and *When We Dead Awaken*.
[4] *The Lady from the Sea*, Act III, p. 273.

36

On the other hand, the previous study has clearly shown Synge to have been perfectly familiar with the use of the symbol as a literary means of expression.[1] In *Riders to the Sea* the old Aran fisherwife grows in stature as her sorrows increase throughout the action of the play, until at the end she is represented as a symbol of all the islanders and their tenacious, unequal struggle against the irresistible forces of Nature.

It is, perhaps, the strong feeling of Destiny pervading *Riders to the Sea* which has led many critics to compare it to the classical drama. Corkery, for instance, says: "The greatness of *Riders to the Sea* lies in this: that it is one of the few modern plays written, and successfully written, in the Greek genre."[2] Lamm (one of the few Swedes who has written about Synge) says in his book on modern drama that there is probably no other contemporary play which, without the slightest deviation from naturalistic technique, conveys so much of the classical atmosphere, with its all-enveloping sense of doom.[3] This is almost equally true of Ibsen's later works which include an impressive number of tragedies of Destiny. They differ, however, from Synge's dramas in one particular respect, namely that either the hero or the heroine sinks beneath the weight of a "tragic guilt" rooted in the past. Sometimes they perish together.

But it is not an indispensable condition of Greek drama that disaster should arise from past misdeeds. A well-known Swedish scholar (Schück) points out that, in a Greek tragedy, the fall of the hero *may* be due to a defect of character—the impetuous Ajax is a case in point—but this is certainly not necessary, and the poet does not emphasize it in any way. Œdipus is irritable and hot-tempered, but his misfortunes are not caused by these defects; they are predestined, like those of Antigone.[4] This might also be said of Bartley in *Riders to the Sea* who certainly does not meet with disaster because he has defied his mother. Thus the flavour of an-

---

[1] See above, p. 21.
[2] Corkery, *op. cit.*, p. 108.
[3] Lamm, *op. cit.*, pp. 311–312.
[4] Henrik Schück, *Illustrerad allmän litteraturhistoria*, vol. I, (Stockholm 1919), pp. 137–138.

tiquity, with the theme of Destiny strongly accentuated, is found in both Synge and Ibsen.

*

There are also several technical peculiarities in *Riders to the Sea* reminiscent of the Ibsenian drama. This is evident in Synge's method of increasing the tension by causing the action to be interrupted as soon as something important is about to be revealed, such as the identity of the owner of the clothes in *Riders to the Sea*, or, in Ibsen's case, the name of "the Stranger" in *The Lady from the Sea*.

Devices of this kind are, of course, common to all dramatists. But they may be adduced as proofs in the case of Synge because his work shows several other technical characteristics usually regarded as peculiar to the Ibsen drama. One is to be found in the extraordinarily clever way in which Ibsen, by the use of parallel scenes, manages to evoke the past. We have already found how he applied this technique in a striking way in *Rosmersholm*, where the final tragedy in the mill-stream is, as it were, a terrible repetition of a suicide which took place before the opening of the drama. Among numerous other instances there is, however, one of particular interest in this connection, namely the last scene of the first act of *Ghosts* (1881). Regina's cry: "Oswald! take care! are you mad? Let me go!" is heard from the next room, immediately after Mrs. Alving has been telling the Reverend Manders how she once caught her own husband and the housemaid in exactly the same situation.[1]

This "ghost scene" has been duly praised. Consequently, it is interesting to notice how Synge uses precisely the same technique in *Riders to the Sea*. In the scene in which old Maurya tells her daughters how, long ago, the sea gave her back one of her dead sons, she says:

> "I was sitting here with Bartley, and he a baby lying on my two knees, and I seen two women, and three women, and four women coming in, and they crossing themselves and not saying a word. I looked out then, and there were men coming after them, and they holding a thing in the half of a red sail, and water dripping out of it—it was a dry day, Nora—and leaving a track to the door."[2]

---

[1] *Ghosts*, Act I (C. W., VII, p. 213).

[2] *Riders to the Sea*, pp. 46–47.

The old woman has hardly finished her vivid description of how one of her drowned sons was brought home, when the shadow of the past begins to haunt the scene as Bartley's home-coming mirrors that of his brother down to the smallest particular.

*

Finally, some mention should perhaps be made of the manner in which Synge differs from Ibsen. In *Riders to the Sea* as in *In the Shadow of the Glen* the differences are primarily due to the fact that the milieu described by Synge, and, consequently, the social position of his chief characters, are so utterly unlike those we find in the works of Ibsen. The people whom the Irish playwright depicts are all inhabitants of the Aran Islands, a group of isolated rocky islands some way out in the Atlantic. In this community, certainly one of the most primitive to be found in Europe, Synge himself lived among the fishermen as one of themselves, sharing their simple fare. He felt instinctively akin to the islanders with their primitive, sometimes almost savage gaiety, which nothing, not even the insatiable sea, is likely to subdue.

Scenes such as the keening of the old people, the herding of cattle, or the arrest of a wrongdoer by the local police, accompanied by vociferous oaths, were almost daily events which had a stimulating effect upon Synge's creative imagination, already highly-developed. A closer study of his plays reveals very clearly to what an extent their construction depends on personal experiences and impressions of such scenes; invaluable sources of inspiration for a responsive artist.

Furthermore, Synge deliberately refrains from drawing any kind of moral conclusions. It is typical of him that he shows no interest whatever in the question as to whether Bartley ought or ought not to have obeyed his mother. As in *In the Shadow of the Glen*, it is for the audience, or the reader, to form an opinion as to the solution of the problem. Thus, once again, we are unmistakably reminded of Ibsen who was accustomed to dispose of importunate questions with the retort: "I prefer to ask, it is not my task to answer."

On the other hand, *Riders to the Sea*, unlike its immediate predecessor, might almost be looked upon as being a play with a purpose. For it is difficult not to feel that, in creating the figure of

Maurya, Synge consciously or unconsciously paid tribute to the hardy fisher-folk, whose joys and sorrows he had made his own, eating their bread and salt and sharing their vigils.

Taken separately it is true that none of the above-mentioned similarities can be said to justify a definite conclusion as to the extent of Ibsen's influence on Synge. However, it is equally true that, placed together, the various parallels drawn above form a body of evidence supporting the theory that the connexion between Synge and his Norwegian predecessor, though hitherto unjustifiably disregarded, is far from negligible.

CHAPTER III

The Tinker's Wedding

The League of Youth

In the opening pages of his travel book *In Wicklow, West Kerry and Connemara* Synge offers his readers a colourful picture of the vagrant's life. "Among the country people of the East of Ireland," he writes, "the tramps and tinkers who wander round from the West have a curious reputation for witchery and unnatural powers."[1] A Wicklow farmer stirs the author's imagination. " 'They come from every part,' he said. 'They're gallous lads for walking round through the world. One time I seen fifty of them above on the road to Rathdangan, and they all match-making and marrying themselves for the year that was to come.' "[2]

This is the background of Synge's only two-act play, *The Tinker's Wedding*, "generally labelled an ugly duckling."[3] So far it has never been enacted in Ireland. The drama, which is modelled on an anecdote told by Synge in his Wicklow sketches,[4] was published in 1908. But according to the author himself it was written "about the time I was working at *Riders to the Sea*, and *In the Shadow of the Glen*. I have re-written it since."[5] The last remark is characteristic of Synge. For "it was his habit, as it was Ibsen's, to go over and over his plays."[6]

*

---

[1] *Op. cit.*, p. 4.
[2] *Ibid.*, p. 5.
[3] David H. Greene, *"The Tinker's Wedding. A Revaluation,"* PMLA, LXII (1947), p. 824.
[4] *Op. cit.*, pp. 47–48.
[5] Note to *The Tinker's Wedding*.
[6] P. P. Howe, *J. M. Synge* (London 1912), p. 92.

The play shows us Michael Byrne, the tinker, being literally dragged to the priest by his doxy, Sarah Casey, to marry her lest he should continue to neglect her, in which case she threatens to ally herself with Jaunting Jim who has "a grand eye for a woman." Much against his will Michael eventually decides to humour her, and they arrange to let a priest marry them for the gallon can the tinker is making, together with the trifle of money they have. During the night, however, his old mother, Mary Byrne, steals the can and immediately "swaps" it in order to quench her permanent thirst in a pint of porter. Next morning the priest discovers the fraud and very naturally refuses to marry the young couple. Michael looses his head and seizes the priest, threatening to plunge him into a bog-hole. In the end the poor man is released, but only after making a solemn promise not to inform the police. Having secured his freedom, the priest, without forswearing himself, hurls a Latin malediction at the tinkers who run for their very lives, leaving him master of the situation.

*

For obvious reasons we must not expect that a play like *The Tinker's Wedding* should afford much material for the student of the possible connexion between Ibsen and Synge. In fact, only one of Ibsen's plays offers a faint resemblance to Synge's wilful little farce, and that is *The League of Youth* (1869). This drama has a very complicated plot which need not detain us here. In our case it is sufficient to point out that much of the play reads like a witty satire upon married life. Man is more or less at the mercy of chance. It does not seem to matter very much with whom one strikes up an acquaintance. The persons of the play change partners almost every hour, turning the whole action into a frivolous farce.

Thus the two plays have in common this general note of "matchmaking" and people "marrying themselves" on the spur of the moment.

Finally, a word or two might be said about Synge's malicious humour. "Critics in general," Bourgeois remarks, "have no hesitancy in branding as un-Irish Synge's sardonic humour."[1] Be

---

[1] Bourgeois, *op. cit.*, p. 217.

that as it may. In any case, the same kind of humour is inherent in quite a number of Ibsen's plays, *e.g. Peer Gynt, The Wild Duck,* and *Hedda Gabler.* An element of pitiless comedy is characteristic of part of the work of both Ibsen and Synge. They share the same tendency of seeing as well as emphasizing the humorous aspects of life even in the most painful situations, which would, no doubt, seem utterly unbearable were it not for the sardonic humour of the two dramatists.

In conclusion it seems safe to maintain that in the case of *The Tinker's Wedding* we had better speak only of possible impressions rather than of actual influence from the Ibsen drama.

CHAPTER IV

The Well of the Saints

The Wild Duck

The Well of the Saints was first performed in February 1905, at the newly-founded Abbey Theatre. Not more than about twenty people made up the first-night audience. After only seven performances the play was removed from the repertoire. Since that date it has never enjoyed any popularity approaching that of the two one-act plays.

*

The action in *The Well of the Saints* takes place in a "lonely mountainous district in the east of Ireland one or more centuries ago." The play is in three acts. When the curtain rises two blind beggars, Martin Doul and his wife Mary, appear to the spectators sitting at the side of the road, waiting for alms. Their blindness has, of course, isolated them from the outer world. But, on the whole, they are contented with the conditions in which they live, as they have created in their own imagination a picture of themselves as a handsome couple. A wandering saint has been told of their plight. By means of water from a holy well he succeeds in restoring their sight. But then the merciless daylight reveals the bitter truth to the beggars, who are heart-broken, indeed almost nauseated, seeing each other old and ugly. Only with the help of the blacksmith's brawny arms the saint is able to prevent the enraged couple from attacking each other.

The second act is staged at Timmy the blacksmith's forge in the village. Now that his sight has been restored, Martin Doul is forced to work for his living like everyone else, and he has reluctantly consented to become the blacksmith's help. However, he seizes every conceivable opportunity of courting Timmy's future bride, lovely Molly Byrne, whose voice charmed him when he was blind. But she only pokes fun at him and threatens to tell his wife of his behaviour. Martin Doul, however, is not easily discouraged. He continues wooing Molly Byrne with sentimental, highfaluting proposals. She as constantly repels the unattractive tatterdemalion in ever more outspoken terms and finally makes an object of derision of the lovesick old man in the presence of the smith and Mary Doul.

The third and last act brings us back to the starting-point. The two beggars have become blind again. Happily re-united in their own darkened world, Martin and Mary Doul now find life as enjoyable as before. Consequently, when the saint returns after a time to offer them a permanent cure, Martin Doul knocks the can with the healing water out of his hand. The two paupers have seen too much of the real world to wish to regain their sight. The saint threatens them with impending doom, and his many supporters advance menacingly towards them. But even in his blindness Martin Doul is strong enough to master the situation and keep the mob at a distance. Hand in hand the blind couple set out for a new future in the south.

*

Even this very brief summary of the plot clearly shows that the principal theme of the play is the conflict between dream and reality. The beggars' imaginary kingdom is dependent for its very existence on the "life-lie" which is its sole foundation. This is an obvious reminder of the Ibsen play which made the term "life-lie" famous throughout the greater part of the world, namely *The Wild Duck*, published in 1884.

The background of Ibsen's play is the lower-middle class home of the photographer Hjalmar Ekdal, his father, his wife Gina, and their daughter Hedvig. Hjalmar is a dreamer who refuses to accept the drab realities of his everyday life. In consequence, he tries to create an atmosphere of great expectations, telling both himself and other people that he is a great inventor whose fame in the future will be on everybody's lips. As a matter of course, this is only vain boasting and Hjalmar's "life-lie" is maintained at the expense of his family. Both Gina and Hedvig are overtaxed with *his* work while the self-styled inventor is lying on his sofa all day inventing nothing whatever except pretexts for doing nothing—indeed, he does not even open any of the learned books he has collected as necessary for his pretended activity as an inventor.

But this is only the initial aspect of the situation. Because, suddenly Hjalmar's old friend, Gregers Werle, the idealistic candidate for truth, turns up and takes a hand in the game. Through him Hjalmar becomes aware of the fact that not only his assumption of superiority but also his marriage, is founded on a lie. For it is not Hjalmar who is the father of Hedvig but old Werle, the merchant. Gregers Werle exposes his own father, hoping that the revelation of the truth will make his friend Hjalmar a free man and his marriage a true one. But his friend's intervention has quite the opposite effect—Hjalmar only feels disgust for his family and decides to leave them. Gina does not take her husband and his desperate step very seriously but Hedvig who adores her "father" and cannot live without his love, commits suicide in despair.

*

The *sens-moral* of the drama is therefore first and foremost that the happiness of human beings is dependent on their being permitted to preserve their illusions. Deprived of their "life-lie" and forced to see reality in its true colours, they can no longer enjoy or endure an existence which suddenly appears to them unbearable.

Thus there is an obvious similarity, as regards subject-matter, between *The Well of the Saints* and *The Wild Duck*. Ibsen's play, like Synge's, is concerned with people who live in an imaginary world of their own making and who have deluded themselves so completely that the slightest attempt to renew their contact with reality must necessarily spell disaster.

Hjalmar Ekdal has hardly found time to express his happiness as a husband and father in the following words: "Our roof may be poor and humble, Gina; but it is home. And with all my heart I say: here dwells my happiness,"[1] when suddenly Gregers Werle

---

[1] *The Wild Duck*, Act II (C. W., VIII, p. 248).

knocks at his door, bringing with him the information which will blow up the foundations of this happiness, the inexorable "claim of the ideal." In the same way, as soon as Synge's blind beggars regain their eyesight, the imaginary world they have constructed with such loving care crumbles to pieces before their eyes. Until then, their only regret was that they were unable to see each other. "I do be thinking in the long nights it'd be a grand thing if we could see ourselves for one hour, or a minute itself, the way we'd know surely we were the finest man and the finest woman of the seven counties of the east."[1]

However painful the operation, their eyes are opened to the hard facts of reality. But truth, which brings freedom to some people, is too overpowering for both Hjalmar Ekdal and the blind couple. "Rob the average man of his life-illusion,[2] and you rob him of his happiness at the same stroke," Ibsen states in *The Wild Duck*.[3] Synge, it is true, does not make any such express declaration. But the entire tenor of his play is in keeping with the message of *The Wild Duck*. When sight is miraculously restored to the blind couple, they at once become aware of each other's ugliness and dirt. The dreams of beauty of their blind period have been formed from earlier memories and from what other people have told them about life and about themselves—in addition to the willed working of their own imagination. "You know rightly," says Mary Doul, speaking of herself, "it was 'the beautiful dark woman' they did call me in Ballinatone."[4] And, again, in the first act it is revealed that she has been mockingly called "the wonder of the western world."[5] Martin Doul, too, has a high opinion of his "outer man." He has overheard the remarks of the young girls: "— — — they do be saying I'm a handsome man,"[6] he states with great satisfaction.

When the scales are removed from their eyes, the beggars are in a cruel manner faced with the world of those who have always

---

[1] *The Well of the Saints*, Act I, pp. 57–58.
[2] Lit. "the life-lie."
[3] *The Wild Duck*, Act V, p. 372.
[4] *The Well of the Saints*, Act I, p. 57.
[5] *Ibid.*, Act I, p. 72.
[6] *Ibid.*, Act I, p. 71.

kept their eyesight, and in this world there seems to be no room for such miserable beings as they are. The discovery of their own ugliness and decayed bodies is the more bitter for Martin Doul and his wife as they cannot but realize that such must long have been the case. All they have been told of their own beauty turns out to be a mere fabrication of jocular and pitiless outsiders who indulged in the pastime of making sport of their vanity, credulity and help-lessness.

The disappointment resulting from their encounter with the visible world and its malice gradually brings the blind couple together again. Under the impression of a cruel reality they cling more closely than ever to their old dreams and illusions in the days when they were still happily living in darkness, "hearing the birds and bees humming in every weed of the ditch, or — — — smelling the sweet, beautiful smell does be rising in the warm nights, when you do hear the swift flying things racing in the air."[1] And so, when the saint appears for the last time in order to open their eyes for ever to the beauty of the earth, Martin Doul, by a symbolical gesture, makes him drop the jug with the miraculous water, bitterly, yet triumphantly contrasting what it has to offer to the joys of his own indestructible dream-world:

"For if it's a right some of you have to be working and sweating the like of Timmy the smith, and a right some of you have to be fasting and praying and talking holy talk the like of yourself, I'm thinking it's a good right ourselves have to be sitting blind, hearing a soft wind turning round the little leaves of the spring and feeling the sun, and we not tormenting our souls with the sight of the gray days, and the holy men, and the dirty feet is trampling the world."[2]

A comparative study of *The Well of the Saints* and Ibsen's *Wild Duck* shows us both plays as concerned with the conflict between reality and illusion. Both Hjalmar Ekdal and the blind couple deliberately create their own dream-world, which they jealously guard against the intrusion of reality. The dream-world of Ibsen's hero is founded on his willed belief in himself as a great inventor as well as a happy husband and father. Synge's two blind people

[1] *The Well of the Saints*, Act III, p. 124.
[2] *Ibid.*, Act III, p. 130.

48

who can neither see nor form any definite judgement on their
surroundings, desperately cling to their dream of beauty concerning
themselves. Thus both dramas present elaborate variations of the
same theme, *i.e.* man's spiritual blindness.

This is followed, in Ibsen's as in Synge's play, by the unveiling
of facts, leading up to practically the same result. Under such
circumstances it is not surprising to find that both dramas end on
a similar note. In each case, we are shown how the principal characters are about to return to their starting-point, *i.e.* the world of
illusion, where "the life-lie" is indispensable to man's happiness.

There is no definite statement in *The Wild Duck* that Hjalmar
Ekdal will again take refuge in one of his many castles in Spain.
As has already been pointed out, Ibsen had contracted the habit of
leaving the future of his characters open to discussion or to the
imagination of his readers. But the words which the dramatist
puts into Relling's mouth just before the end of the play: "Before
a year is over, little Hedvig will be nothing to him but a pretty
theme for declamation,"[1] justify the opinion that the author must
have had some such solution in mind.

The essential feature of the argument is, however, that both
Ibsen and Synge consider illusion and self-deception to be far more
important to human happiness than a disillusioned recognition of
the truth. Thus the juxtaposition of the two plays clearly shows
The Well of the Saints to have been composed on much the same
lines as Ibsen's drama of "the life-lie." A close examination of the
details in the former play reveals a few interesting points reminiscent of *The Wild Duck*. First of all, Ibsen's drama is also concerned
with blindness, both physical and spiritual. Furthermore, Synge
follows the Ibsenian tradition when he adopts the name of Doul
for the blind couple, a slight alteration of the Irish word "dall,"
meaning "blind."[2]

All through his life Ibsen devoted a great deal of thought and
care to the choice of names for the off-spring of his brain, especially
favouring those that had a symbolical significance. Even in his
earliest drama, *Catilina*, published in 1850, he altered the "Fulvia"

---

[1] *The Wild Duck*, Act V, p. 399.
[2] Corkery, *op. cit.*, p. 153, note.

of his sources to the impressive "Furia."[1] Similar changes of names are extremely common in his works after *Catilina*. It may here be mentioned that the heroine in *The Lady from the Sea* was originally called "Thora." Later on Ibsen substituted for this name "Ellida" which he had hit upon in *Frithiof's Saga* where it is applied to a ship. Such a name, Koht points out, is indeed far more reminiscent of storm and secret magic[2] than is the uninteresting "Thora."

Ibsen is, of course, not the only author who uses symbol names for his characters. On the contrary the same device is frequently resorted to in modern drama. But in a comparative study of Ibsen and Synge it may not be without interest to establish the fact that both dramatists make use of this highly effective means of literary expression.

A closer analysis reveals several minor similarities between the chief characters in both dramas. Like Synge's blind couple Hjalmar Ekdal shows an inherent tendency of talking himself into believing in his own pretences and of indulging in day-dreams which cannot possibly be reconciled to naked facts. Yet it is often difficult to ascertain whether these people really believe in the heroic part they play with such admirable skill. Hjalmar Ekdal, for instance, is not always quite sure of his future success as an inventor. He is, in fact, painfully aware of the great expectations entertained by his family. The best instance of this fact is to be found in his frequent excuses and evasions whenever the subject of his inventions is broached. Finally he admits to Gregers Werle that he can no longer believe in them: "Why, great heavens, what would you have me invent? Other people have invented almost everything already. It becomes more and more difficult every day—"[3]

Similarly, the dream of beauty which lends colour and charm to Martin Doul's life, occasionally seems also to him but an illusion. Witness the following expressive words to his wife: "I do be thinking odd times we don't know rightly what way you have your splendour, or asking myself, maybe, if you have it at all, for the

---

[1] Kehler, *op. cit.*, p. 93.
[2] Koht, *op. cit.*, vol. II, p. 281.
[3] *The Wild Duck*, Act V, p. 387.

time I was a young lad, and had fine sight, it was the ones with sweet voices were the best in face."[1]

*

However, *The Well of the Saints*, like Synge's earlier plays, differs in certain respects from similar work of Ibsen. The most obvious of these differences are those caused by Synge's choice of time and place, and by the social position of his chief characters. The poetic language in which *The Well of the Saints* is clothed has no counterpart in the later works of Ibsen. The master who wrote *Peer Gynt* was debarred by his new choice of subjects from emphasizing, as Synge does, the poetic ardour of the countryfolk, their sense of humour, coupled with their almost savage delight in the burlesque aspect of life, all of which is a sign of realism in the imagination of the Irish.

Synge's un-Ibsenian method of character drawing in *The Well of the Saints* may be attributed to the fact that he conceived the play as a dramatized myth or legend. Hjalmar and Gina Ekdal on one side and Martin and Mary Doul on the other have nothing whatever in common with each other except their "life-lie" and its consequences. Gregers Werle and the Saint, it is true, are inspired by the same motive, namely to open the eyes of others to what they consider a higher form of existence. But there is no other resemblance between them. Ibsen's Gregers Werle with his "claim of the ideal" is, after all, an autobiographical confession of deep and tragic import, whereas the Saint in Synge's play is nothing but a stage contrivance, a *deus ex machina*, looked on with superstitious awe by the common country folk. Indeed, there are no "saints" of this kind to be found in the writings of Ibsen. In fact, Synge himself does not appear to have felt any particular interest in the Saint as an individual; he simply moves him from place to place like a chess-figure.

However, despite differences, the impression remains that Synge in writing *The Well of the Saints* has tackled a typical Ibsen problem. Throughout the entire action of Synge's drama the central question is the fatal part played by the "life-lie" in the existence of average

[1] *The Well of the Saints*, Act I, p. 56.

and poor people. The problem is also formulated by Synge in a manner closely akin to that used in *The Wild Duck*. Finally, he has arrived at the same conclusion as that drawn by Ibsen, namely that man cannot do without his illusions: "Rob the average man of his life-lie, and you rob him of his happiness at the same stroke!"

CHAPTER V

The Playboy of the Western World

Peer Gynt
The Wild Duck
The Master Builder

In the year 1907 public interest was again focussed on Synge after the first-night performance of his best-known play, *The Playboy of the Western World*.

As he had so often done before, Synge took his subject-matter from an actual occurrence recorded in his travel-sketches in *The Aran Islands*. The story runs as follows:

"Another old man, the oldest on the island, is fond of telling me anecdotes—not folktales—of things that have happened here in his lifetime.

He often tells me about a Connaught man who killed his father with the blow of a spade when he was in a passion, and then fled to this island and threw himself on the mercy of some of the natives with whom he was said to be related. They hid him in a hole—which the old man has shown me—and kept him safe for weeks, though the police came and searched for him, and he could hear their boots grinding on the stones over his head. In spite of a reward which was offered, the island was incorruptible, and after much trouble the man was safely shipped to America."[1]

Unlike the islanders, Synge, in his play, certainly did not connive at the murderer's escape. On the contrary, he allowed justice to take its course. But the staging of a drama in which a son loudly and frequently boasts of having killed his old father was, of course, quite enough to shock public opinion in those days. Further references to the reception given to *The Playboy* will appear later in

---

[1] Synge, *op. cit.*, p. 88.

the analysis; at this point a short account of the chief incidents may
be of use.

*

The background of the drama is a small wayside public-house
or shebeen, on the wild coast of Mayo. The landlord, Michael
James Flaherty, slightly drunk as usual, is preparing to join in a
wake at midnight, leaving his daughter, Pegeen Mike, alone in the
house. She has, it is true, an admirer in her cousin, Shawn Keogh.
But he is far too much in awe of the Church, as personified by
Father Reilly, to dream of spending a night alone with his future
wife. Consequently, when a mysterious stranger suddenly appears
on the scene, Pegeen is prepared at once to transfer her interest
and affections to him. The visitor becomes still more interesting to
her shortly afterwards, when he inadvertently confesses to the
murder of his father. The newcomer turns out to be Christy Mahon,
the hero of the play. Hunted by the police, he has now taken refuge
in the public-house, hoping to find a hiding-place from his pursuers.
The young boy scores an unexpected success, as the fanciful story
he tells about himself immediately makes him a popular hero. The
women at once start fighting each other for his sake and the landlord engages him as a pot-boy. Christy Mahon, formerly the timid,
silent and subdued victim of his father's tyranny, is readily made
aware of his own latent potentialities by the reactions of his newly
acquired friends. Thus, when the curtain falls at the end of the
first act, the young hero is feeling extremely pleased with himself
as he makes his preparations for the night in the little inn, with
the once-proud daughter of the house now honoured by the presence of such a guest sleeping in the next room.

During the following act, Christy's star is still in the ascendant.
The girls of the neighbourhood have no eyes for anyone but the
stranger; they swarm about him, eager to hear more of his savage
deed. Their keen attention and the many generous gifts they be-
stow upon him, encourages Christy to re-tell his story over and
over again, adding further exciting details with each repetition.
"That's a grand story," they say. "He tells it lovely." Their reaction
is all the more violent when, just as Christy is telling them how
he "cleft his father with one blow to the breeches belt," the spectral

figure of old Mahon himself, with his head "in a mass of bandages and plaster," appears upon the scene! Christy makes a hairbreadth escape, while the lovesick, though materially-minded, Widow Quin holds the fort and succeeds in getting rid of the "dead" man by giving him a false trail to follow in his search for his good-for-nothing son. As soon as his father has gone, she tries to convince Christy that she would make a suitable wife for him. Unwillingly forced to acknowledge the fact that he cares for no one but Pegeen, the widow changes her mind and even offers to help Christy to win the girl he has set his heart on, if he will reward her lavishly in kind. Their conversation is suddenly brought to an end by the arrival of a group of girls who, with Pegeen as their chief attraction, induce Christy to come with them to the athletic contests which are to be held in the village.

At the beginning of the third and last act Christy has attained still greater fame and glory as winner of the races on the beach. Followed by his admirers "the champion Playboy of the Western World" returns in a triumphal procession from the scene of his victories. Christy has attained his goal; weighed down beneath the prizes he has accumulated, he is now accepted by Pegeen as her hero. "You are the lad," she says to him as soon as they are alone together, whereupon they proceed to confess their love of each other in highflown language. But just as her father, the landlord, is about to give them his blessing, who should arrive on the scene but the "dead" Mahon. This time he succeeds in capturing his son, and he administers a sound thrashing to him which effectively deprives Christy of his heroic nimbus and makes it impossible for the credulous villagers ever to be deceived by him again. But at the same time another change has happened to the boy; for he is no longer prepared meekly to accept punishment from his father. In a desperate attempt to regain his former prestige, he aims a stunning blow at the old man, in order to fulfill the deed, the mere mention of which had earlier sufficed to make him a hero in the eyes of the villagers. But this new act of violence has exactly the opposite effect. Without the softening effect of distance to make the story seem as remote as that of Jack the Giant-Killer, the sordid light of reality shows it to be a brutal and repulsive crime. "There's a great gap," says Pegeen, "between a gallous story and a dirty deed." Christy is actually about to be lynched, when his father, showing no traces of further injury, most unexpectedly makes his appearance, crawling on hands and knees, to save the "hero." For the poor man cannot quite conceal the pride and joy he feels at the "manly courage" shown by the once-craven Christy in his two attempts to kill his own father! And so old Mahon and his son turn their backs upon the angry villagers, leaving Pegeen to mourn her shattered illusions.

*

If the reader of the above summary now turns to Ibsen, it will soon be apparent that more than one of his plays may well have sponsored *The Playboy*. A chronological account should begin with *Peer Gynt*. As this drama, ever since its publication in 1867, has been well-known to most European readers, a description of the plot would probably be a work of supererogation. As an alternative, a summary account of the order in which the scenes are arranged may be useful.

Act I.

Peer Gynt's story of the adventurous ride on the goat's back.—The meeting with Solveig.—The tale of the Devil in the nut.—The abduction of the bride.

Act II.

Peer Gynt deserts the bride.—The episode of the Saeter-girls.—Peer Gynt and the Green-Clad Woman.—In the hall of the Dovre-King.—Peer Gynt and the Boyg.

Act III.

The parting from Solveig caused by the return of the Green-Clad Woman with her child by Peer Gynt.—The death of Åse.

Act IV.

In Morocco; the yacht-episode.—The episode of Anitra and the Prophet.—Peer Gynt as a historian. In Egypt: the Sphinx and the Echo.—The Asylum in Cairo.

Act V.

Peer Gynt's voyage home.—The strange Passenger.—The priest's sermon on the conscientious objector who was, however, "true to himself."—The auction at Haegstad.—The incident of the onion without

56

a kernel.—Peer Gynt's mental agony.—The episode of the thread-balls and the withered leaves.—The Button Moulder.—Peer Gynt's insight as to the right way, and his confession of his sins.—The triumph of love!

Another point which should not be overlooked in this connection is the fact that the entire drama of Peer Gynt is founded on the contrast between the troll-motto: "Troll, to thyself be—enough!" and the true human one: "Man, be thyself!" There is also the conflict between the doctrine of "the Boyg:" "Go roundabout!" as opposed to the moral commandment: "Right through!"

*

If Peer Gynt is kept in mind during an analysis of the figure of Christy Mahon, many aspects worthy of attention will appear in a new light.

To begin with, both Peer Gynt and Christy Mahon are blessed with a vivid imagination and a youthful charm which deflect attention from their faults making them irresistible to women. It may be of interest, *à propos* this subject, to dwell for a moment upon one of the central scenes of *The Playboy*, which appears somewhat reminiscent of *Peer Gynt*. When the report of Christy's deed of violence is spread in the neighbourhood, he immediately becomes the centre of attraction for three country girls who vie with and outbid each other in their eagerness to start a flirtation with the daring hero.[1]

As for Peer Gynt, it so happens that he has just carried away the bride by force at the time of his encounter with the three wild saetergirls. "If lads are awanting," cries one of the girls, "one plays with the trolls!"[2] Peer Gynt regards these words as a challenge and he at once begins to boast. "I'm a three-headed troll," he exclaims, "and the boy for three girls!"[3] The curiosity of the girls is immediately aroused and the trolls are forgotten, as they cluster round Peer Gynt—one is even bold enough to give him a kiss. Finally, the girls make mocking gestures at the mountain-tops and dance away with Per Gynt in their midst.

---

[1] *The Playboy of the Western World*, Act II: introductory scene.
[2] *Peer Gynt*, Act II: 3 (C. W., IV, p. 61).
[3] *Ibid.*

A further comparison between Peer Gynt and Christy Mahon
shows them both to have risen from humble circumstances to become respectable members of society by the simple process of
transforming the dreary truths of their everyday life into brilliant
and colourful lies. As Bourgeois very aptly remarks:

"Like all great poets, Christy Mahon is a liar of genius or, at the very
least, an embroiderer, in the true lineal descent of Corneille's Dorante,
Daudet's Tartarin, Ibsen's Peer Gynt, and Rostand's Cyrano. 'It is
humbugging us he is.' Like all these masters, Synge personifies in
his hero the romance inherent in sheer mendacity. Like all his pre-
decessors in European drama, Christy Mahon at first believes in his
own lie, and, 'in the end of all,' falls a victim to it."[1]

In other words, both *Peer Gynt* and *The Playboy* deal with
heroes who rebel against the despotism of reality, because they
refuse to submit to the tyrannical rules of everyday existence.
Indeed, the very first words in *Peer Gynt*, Mother Åse's angry,
protesting "Peer, you are lying!" skilfully introduce one of the central themes of the drama.

Furthermore, Peer Gynt and Christy both have the braggart's
tendency to lose his head at the slightest hint of danger. Peer
Gynt's sudden change of mood when he has escaped from being
drowned with his "friends" in the wreck of the yacht illustrates
this propensity.

PEER GYNT. What a marvellous feeling of safety and peace
It gives one to know oneself specially shielded!
But the desert! What about food and drink?
Oh, something I'm sure to find. *He*'ll see to that.
There's no cause for alarm;—(*Loud and insinuatingly.*)
                                        He would never allow
A poor little sparrow like me to perish!
Be but lowly of spirit. And give him time.
Leave it all in the Lord's hands; and don't be cast down.—(*With a
start of terror.*)
Can that be a lion that growled in the reeds—? (*His teeth chattering.*)
No, it wasn't a lion. (*Mustering up courage.*)
A lion, forsooth![2]

In the first act of *The Playboy* Synge has a similar scene which
exposes with equal ruthlessness the fundamental cowardice beneath

[1] Bourgeois, *op. cit.*, p. 205.　　[2] *Peer Gynt*, Act IV: 2, p. 142.

Christy's braggadocio. A sudden knock at the door pricks the bubble
of his reputation:

PEGEEN (*putting her hand on his shoulder*).
Well, you'll have peace in this place, Christy Mahon, and none to
trouble you, and it's near time a fine lad like you should have your
good share of the earth.
CHRISTY. It's time surely, and I a seemly fellow with great strength in
me and bravery of ... (*Some one knocks*).
CHRISTY (*clinging to Pegeen*). Oh, glory! it's late for knocking, and this
last while I'm in terror of the peelers, and the walking dead.[1]

The Irish hero shares Peer Gynt's inability to distinguish between lies and pure fiction or rather the products of an abundant
imagination. When, in the last act of the play, Peer Gynt comes
home again, nobody recognizes him, and he is surprised to hear
that he is known in the neighbourhood as "an abominable liar."[2]
When he asks for an explanation the bailiff replies:

Yes—all that was strong and great
He made believe always that *he* had done it.[3]

Pegeen, in like manner, feels that Christy's fantastic stories are
inspired by his poetic gifts. Hence her comment on his deed:

I've heard all times it's the poets are your like—
fine, fiery fellows with great rages when their temper's
roused.[4]

Two other equally illuminating remarks are made by Pegeen in
the last act:

— — — any girl would walk her heart out before she'd
meet a young man was your like for eloquence, or talk at all.[5]

And

—what is it I have, Christy Mahon, to make me
fitting entertainment for the like of you, that
has such poet's talking, and such bravery of heart.[6]

---

[1] *The Playboy of the Western World*, Act I, p. 34.
[2] *Peer Gynt*, Act V: 4, p. 224. "Digter"; means also "poet." (Translator's note.)
[3] *Ibid.*
[4] *The Playboy of the Western World*, Act I, p. 30.
[5] *Ibid.*, Act III, p. 90.
[6] *Ibid.*, Act III, p. 91.

Much of the charm of *Peer Gynt* may be ascribed to the skill with which fact and fantasy are woven together into an exquisite, colourful tapestry. Peer Gynt himself is perfectly well equipped to play the part of the boy who challenges the giant to an eating-contest, or indeed to be the hero of any other well-known fairy-tale. Christy, it is true, differs from Peer Gynt in so far as he has nothing to do with the trolls and their like. But he undoubtedly behaves exactly as though he were the boy who had slain the ogre. Synge, like Ibsen, on the whole adds many touches to the portrait of his hero which make his identification an obvious matter for a Scandinavian, familiar since childhood with the stories of many boisterous good-for-nothings of the past who became popular heroes by committing acts of violence. Ibsen's peasants, like Synge's, are fascinated by all kinds of adventure, myth and saga. The numerous exploits of Peer Gynt (*e.g.* the daring ride on the goat's back and the Devil in the nut) are simply the outcome of unrestrained flights of fancy. Christy, too, allows his imagination to run away with him, so that the particulars of his crime become more and more grotesque.

Thus, both Ibsen's and Synge's heroes are born story-tellers who seem to be able to make even their wildest inventions acceptable. Moreover, if a woman takes them seriously, they are at once ready to confess their love for her in the most ardent terms. Having in mind their poetic gifts, this is only to be expected. But it is, nevertheless, an interesting coincidence that some of the loveliest lyrical passages in *Peer Gynt* are to be found in the scenes between Peer and Solveig. This may also be said of the love-dialogue spoken by Christy and Pegeen, which is truly unique.

But a romantic strain and a propensity for lying are by no means the only qualities shared by Christy and Peer Gynt. Curiously enough, they are both at times able to take a realistic view of life. Thus, Peer Gynt, although he is a dreamer, turns out to be practical enough to establish himself as a ship-owner on a large scale. Christy, too, has a sharp eye to the main chance. The last words of the first act and the introductory scene of the second might be described as "the portrait of a potential social-climber."

Well, it's a clean bed and soft with it, and it's great luck and company I've won me in the end of time—two fine women fighting for the likes of me—till I'm thinking this night wasn't I a foolish fellow not to kill my father in the years gone by.[1]

And then:

Well, this'd be a fine place to be my whole life talking out with swearing Christians, in place of my old dogs and cat; and I stalking around, smoking my pipe and drinking my fill, and never a day's work but drawing a cork an odd time, or wiping a glass, or rinsing out a shiny tumbler for a decent man.[2]

The social background of Ibsen's play, quite unexpectedly, is the same as that of Synge's, both plays being peasant-dramas. The ramifications of the plot in each case are of a kind scarcely possible in any but the most primitive milieu.

Moreover, both Peer Gynt and Christy are country lads who take every conceivable opportunity of boasting about their forefathers. Warming to the subject, Peer Gynt, expresses himself as follows:

> Peace, mother; what need we care!
> 'Tis the rich Jon Gynt gives the banquet;
> Hurrah for the race of Gynt!
> ⸻
> Peer Gynt, thou art come of great things,
> And great things shall come of thee![3]

"The Playboy" is equally emphatic:

CHRISTY (with a flash of family pride). And I the son of a strong farmer (with a sudden qualm), God rest his soul, could have bought up the whole of your old house a while since, from the butt of his tailpocket, and not have missed the weight of it gone.[4]

And when Pegeen sings the praises of Christy's great ancestors, the young impostor proudly joins in:

We were great, surely, with wide and windy acres of rich Munster land.[5]

The real motive for both Peer Gynt's and "the Playboy"'s revolt

[1] The Playboy of the Western World, Act 1, p. 41.
[2] Ibid., Act II, pp. 42–43.
[3] Peer Gynt, Act II: 5, p. 65.
[4] The Playboy of the Western World, Act I, p. 19.
[5] Ibid., Act I, p. 28.

against the tyranny of stubborn facts is that they are both unable
to conform to the standards of their neighbours. Peer Gynt feels
like a prisoner in the valley, where everyone looks down upon him:

> Yonder sail two brown eagles.
> Southward the wild geese fly.
> And here I must splash and stumble
> In quagmire and filth knee-deep!
>
> *(Springs up.)*
> I'll fly too! I will wash myself clean in
> The bath of the keenest winds!
> I'll fly high![1]

Christy is the helpless victim of a tyrannical old father, who
makes his life a misery to him.

CHRISTY (*laughing piteously*). The like of a king, is it? And I after toiling,
moiling, digging, dodging from the dawn till dusk; with never a sight
of joy or sport saving only when I'd be abroad in the dark night poach-
ing rabbits on hills — — —.[2]

And again:

— — — and he a man never gave peace to any, saving when he'd
get two months or three, or be locked in the asylums for battering
peelers or assaulting men (*with depression*), the way it was a bitter
life he led me till I did up a Tuesday and halve his skull.[3]

Finally, when the tension has become unendurable, both react
by committing a deed of violence. Thus, Peer Gynt abducts the
bride, and Christy, as he thinks, slays his father.

Christy Mahon and Peer Gynt also share a tendency to invoke
the aid of the Almighty even in the most trivial matters. Peer Gynt
has presumably inherited this habit from his mother, Åse, who
hardly ever utters a sentence without taking God's name in vain.
Neither Peer Gynt nor "the Playboy" hesitate to "trouble" the
Lord whenever they find themselves in difficulties.

When Peer Gynt's yacht is stolen, he raises his hands in prayer
to God to stop the thieves. But the wording of his prayer clearly
reveals his all-comprehensive egotism:

"It is *I*, Peter Gynt! Oh, our Lord, give but heed!"[4]

---

[1] *Peer Gynt*, Act II: 5, p. 64.
[2] *The Playboy of the Western World*, Act I, p. 32.
[3] *Ibid.*, Act I, pp. 33–34.   [4] *Peer Gynt*, Act IV: 2, p. 141.

In like manner, Christy Mahon can draw on seemingly inexhaustible reserves of prayer and piety, in order to further his own interests:

> Aid me for to win Pegeen. It's herself only that I'm seeking now. —— Aid me for to win her, and I'll be asking God to stretch a hand to you in the hour of death, and lead you short cuts through the Meadows of Ease, and up the floor of Heaven to the Footstool of the Virgin's Son."[1]

But when, in the last act, Christy has worked himself up to one of these perorations, he is severely snubbed by his father. The moment his son raises his hands for an impressive "In the name of the Almighty God," old Mahon silences him with the words: "Leave troubling the Lord God."[2]

It should, perhaps, be mentioned that this repeated misuse of the name of God was a contributory cause of the violent demonstrations against Synge's literary *enfant terrible*.

Still another important resemblance between *Peer Gynt* and *The Playboy* calls for attention, namely, the purpose of both plays. As is already well known, each of these works created violent animosity and met with bitter opposition in its native country. The Norwegian drama, like the Irish one, was regarded as a ferocious satire and an unpatriotic mockery of the author's countrymen. Both writers ably defended themselves against their detractors. In a letter to his publisher, Ibsen wrote:

> "I learn that the book (*i.e. Peer Gynt*) has created much excitement in Norway. This does not trouble me in the least; but both there and in Denmark they have discovered much more satire in it than was intended by me. Why can they not read the book as a poem? For as such I wrote it. The satirical passages are tolerably isolated. But if the Norwegians of the present time recognise themselves, as it would appear they do, in the character of Peer Gynt, that is the good people's own affair."[3]

It will readily be understood that these sentences might almost equally well have been written by Synge. But the latter, unlike

---

[1] *The Playboy of the Western World*, Act II, p. 73.

[2] *Ibid.*, Act III, p. 102.

[3] Henrik Ibsen to Frederik Hegel, 24th February 1868. Quoted from William Archer's introduction to *Peer Gynt*.

Ibsen, who had then safely settled in Rome, permitted the heat of the battle to provoke him to utterances that unfortunately were less discreet than the lines written by the Norwegian poet. In a letter to a Dublin paper Synge declared:

> "*The Playboy of the Western World* is not a play with a 'purpose' in the modern sense of the word, but, although parts of it are or are meant to be extravagant comedy, still a great deal that is in it and a great deal more that is behind it is perfectly serious when looked at in a certain light. This is often the case, I think, with comedy, and no one is quite sure to-day whether Shylock or Alceste should be played seriously or not. There are, it may be hinted, several sides to the *Playboy*."[1]

As we have already seen above, much of the prefaces to Synge's plays reads like a conscious attack upon Ibsen. It is, however, particularly remarkable that he should have sought in vain for "humour," "joy" and "poetry" in the works of the Norwegian master. Such an opinion cannot be accepted without deliberately ignoring *Peer Gynt*, to mention only the most obvious example. Indeed, any attempt to overlook the joyful and humorous as well as poetic aspects which are part and parcel of this intricate play would be a failure.[2]

Synge evidently overrated his countrymen's sense of humour and Ibsen apparently made the same mistake about the Norwegians. "I do not think," wrote Synge, "that these country people, who have so much humour themselves, will mind being laughed at without malice, as the people in every country have been laughed at in their own comedies."[3] The satirical element, however, in both *Peer Gynt* and *The Playboy* is evident at first sight, despite the protests of their authors. In fact, the two plays contain many scenes which must be interpreted as more or less deliberate satire upon national foibles.

As has already been pointed out by other scholars, parallels have been found between Synge's hero and other inveterate story-tellers, generally of French origin. Sometimes even the name of

---

[1] Bourgeois, *op. cit.*, p. 208.
[2] The very word "livsglæde," lit. "life-joy," is known in Scandinavia to have been coined by Ibsen. (See *Ghosts*.)
[3] *Preface* to *The Tinker's Wedding*.

Don Quixote has been mentioned in this context. But having in mind the Irish dramatist's responsive attitude towards contemporary literature, it seems, in view of the above analysis, much more probable that Synge's treatment of the original story of *The Playboy* was conditioned by his impressions of *Peer Gynt*. In Ibsen's hero, with his sudden changes of mood, his excitability, his incapacity of distinguishing between right and wrong, fact and fancy, Synge must certainly have recognized the playboy of his own drama.

Synge himself, it is true, was no "Playboy." Nor was Ibsen a Peer Gynt. Both playwrights were readers and "thinkers," rather than men of action. But this would not prevent either of them from feeling akin to his hero. It is significant that about ten years after the publication of *Peer Gynt* Ibsen wrote a well-known lyric which expresses in four concentrated lines the tragic conflict within himself which embittered his life and inspired most of his writings:

> To *live* is to war with the troll
> In the caverns of heart and of skull.
> To *write poetry*—that is to hold
> Doom-session upon the soul.[1]

The great love which both Ibsen and Synge bore their own people gave them the strength and the courage to reveal what they considered to be the faults and follies of their fellow-countrymen in the full glare of the footlights.

An ironic reflection is cast on the fanatical opposition displayed towards both *Peer Gynt* and *The Playboy* by the nationalists of their respective countries when we take into consideration that few, if any, plays are more calculated to stimulate interest in Norway and Ireland.

*

Peer Gynt's temperament is akin to that of another "daydreamer," Hjalmar Ekdal. The influence of *The Wild Duck* on *The*

---

[1] At *leve* er krig med trolde
i hjertets og hjernens hvælv.
At *digte*, det er at holde
dommedag over sig selv.
Translated by Miss M. C. Bradbrook. See her book *Ibsen the Norwegian. A Revaluation* (London 1946), p. 16.

Well of the Saints has already been established in this analysis. Similarly it is by no means unlikely that Synge may have found inspiration for his portrayal of Christy Mahon in the figure of Hjalmar Ekdal, the extreme egoist who, like Peer Gynt, adopts the motto: "To thyself be—enough!" It is significant that each of these "heroes" perceives his private universe disintegrating before his eyes when the "life-lie" on which it was founded is snatched from him. *The Playboy of the Western World, The Well of the Saints* and *The Wild Duck* are all concerned with the dominant influence of the "life-lie." Christy and Pegeen, like Hjalmar Ekdal, are both given to self-deception. But whereas Ibsen, in the case of Hjalmar Ekdal, shows the preservative properties of the "life-lie," Synge represents its magical power to awaken the better traits of human nature. The arrogant, high-strung attitude of Pegeen melts away and her natural womanly gentleness shines forth in its stead. The surprise she feels at this transformation is exquisitely phrased by Synge:

> And to think it's me is talking sweetly, Christy Mahon, and I the fright of seven townlands for my biting tongue. Well, the heart's a wonder; and I'm thinking, there won't be our like in Mayo, for gallant lovers, from this hour to-day.[1]

Christy, too, when treated like a hero and made the cynosure of all eyes, beats all his competitors on the sports ground. His father's tyranny had isolated him and made him clumsy, silent and timid. Now his new-found eloquence and lyrical intensity threaten the well-knit balance of the play.

There are also technical points of similarity between Synge's play and the Ibsen drama. *The Playboy*, like the problem plays of Ibsen, culminates in a disclosure, and Synge, like Ibsen, concentrates his attention upon the *dénouement*. It is the final stage in a logical sequence of postulates, each carefully planned and demonstrated to the audience in the course of the play.

*

But *Peer Gynt* and *The Wild Duck* are probably not the only Ibsen-dramas which might have had a formative influence upon

---

[1] *The Playboy of the Western World*, Act III, p. 93.

the creator of *The Playboy*. It so happens that Synge's play shows
many resemblances, both thematic and scenic, to *The Master
Builder* (1892), one of Ibsen's most significant dramas.

The central figure of this play is an architect whose overweening ambition causes him to sacrifice other people's happiness in
order to become a leader in his profession. As a matter of fact,
Solness himself states that at the outset of his career he wished to
serve God by building church after church, in the hopes of thus
finding the peace and happiness he craved for. But when, on the
contrary, God visited his wrath on Solness' family, it was revealed
to the Builder that his children had been taken from him so that
he should not fix his affections on any earthly object, for in this life
he was to be God's Master Builder.

Although subject to severe attacks of vertigo, Solness is now no
longer afraid of attempting that which he had formerly regarded as
impossible. He climbs to the top of the church-tower, holding the
ceremonial garland, and from its height delivers his challenge to
God: "Hear me now, thou Mighty One! From this day forward I
will be a free builder—I too, in my sphere—just as thou in thine.
I will never more build churches for thee—only homes for human
beings."[1] But from now on the Master Builder is no longer the
kind of artist God has meant him to be. It soon turns out that the
people who live in his newly-built houses are no happier than
Solness' own family. Thus Ibsen accuses him of building "houses"
rather than "homes."

However, the strong and pitiless Master Builder who allows no
one to impede his rise to fame, has one chink in his armour. He
is afraid of losing his "luck" and dreads the catastrophe he feels
to be inevitable as a result of his challenge to God. His fear and
dread are focussed on the younger generation. He is convinced that
from their ranks will come the victor destined to force him to
withdraw from the arena. "Yes, just you see, doctor—," Solness
says to his friend, "presently the younger generation will come
knocking at my door—"[2] He has scarcely uttered these prophetic
words, when the young girl Hilde Wangel arrives on the scene.
Solness, it appears, had played with her when she was a child and

---

[1] *The Master Builder*, Act III (C. W., X, p. 353).
[2] *Ibid.*, Act I, p. 224.

jokingly promised to come and fetch her ten years later. As Solness did not remember his promise, the "princess," as he used to call her, has now come in person to claim her "kingdom."

There is a marked contrast between Solness, who has a "sickly conscience" towards his fellow-men, and the youthful Hilde, whose conscience is described by Ibsen as "robust."[1] The impression she makes on the ageing Master Builder, whose self-confidence is slipping from him—he builds only houses nowadays, not churches— is as violent and disturbing as though she were a manifestation of the forces of Nature. Hilde Wangel regards Solness as predestined to be her hero, and consequently refuses to admit the possibility of his suffering from any human imperfection. Her subtle questioning whether "*my* master builder *dares* not—*cannot*—climb as high as he builds?"[2] forces Solness to attempt "the *impossible* once again!"[3]

In his final revolt against God, Whom Hilde hears him haranguing from his stand on the scaffolding, Solness climbs to the highest point of his newly-built house. But this time the price of his daring exploit is his life.

*

The extraordinary plot of *The Master Builder*—a play so lacking in external "drama" that it can scarcely be said to have any plot at all—does not appear to have any points of resemblance to *The Playboy*. It must indeed be conceded that at first sight there seems to be much more dissimilarity than likeness between the two plays. With the exception of their different backgrounds, occasioned by Synge's choice of theme, the principal divergence is that *The Master Builder* tells us of an elderly man, who, feeling that life has passed him by, tries to win a young girl, and of the conflict which ensues; whereas the couple in *The Playboy* are "birds of a feather."

But with these notable exceptions, the disparities may on the whole be described as more apparent than real. Although Synge appears to have transposed a typical Ibsenian theme from tragedy

---

[1] *The Master Builder*, Act II, p. 298.
[2] *Ibid.*, Act II, p. 315.
[3] *Ibid.*, Act III, p. 356.

68

to comedy, or rather tragi-comedy, the plays run practically the
same course. In *The Master Builder*, as in *The Playboy*, a woman's
ruthless egotism and excessive admiration of her hero bring about
his downfall, after a hopeless attempt to live up to her precon-
ceived opinion of him. The final scene of *The Playboy* forms a
striking parallel to that of *The Master Builder;* in each case the
hero is dethroned and the young woman left to mourn her loss
and disappointment in utter solitude.

The Master Builder, like *The Playboy*, depicts a young girl whose
hero-worship has become an obsession. Both girls expect their lovers
to conduct themselves like heroes of romance, regardless of consequences. "Do you want to kill me?" cries Hilde. "To take from
me what is more than my life?

SOLNESS. And what is that?

HILDE. The longing to see you great."[1]

It has already been observed, that, when Christy is treated as a
hero, he acts like one. This is also true of Solness. He admits that
he is afraid of climbing on to his scaffolding,[2] but egged on by
Hilde's words his fear is overcome and he regains his self-confidence. A final effort brings him, literally, to the pinnacle of his
achievement.

During the action of each play the heroine, too, experiences a
similar change of heart. Pegeen's naive astonishment at the transformation wrought in her by her love for Christy[3] is mirrored in
some of the last words spoken by Hilde to the Master Builder:

HILDE. Now I see you again as I did when there was song in the air!

SOLNESS. How have you become what you are, Hilda?

HILDE. How have you made me what I am?[4]

Furthermore, Hilde and Pegeen are both gamblers, enjoying
their game all the more because they know the odds are against
them. Hilde Wangel is almost unbearably excited by her uncer-
tainty as to the effect of the forces she has set in motion. This

---

[1] *The Master Builder*, Act II, p. 307.

[2] *Ibid.*, Act III, p. 349.

[3] And to think it's me is talking sweetly, Christy Mahon, and I the fright
of seven townlands for my biting tongue. Well, the heart's a wonder." (*The Playboy of the Western World*, Act III, p. 93.)

[4] *The Master Builder*, Act III, p. 357.

mood is, perhaps, most clearly expressed in her last words in the second act: "frightfully thrilling."[1] But it is also perceptible in the following outburst: "Why should not *I* go a-hunting—I, as well as the rest? Carry off the prey I want—if only I can get my claws into it, and do with it as I will."[2]

On her part, Pegeen is also rather uncertain as to the outcome of her experiment with Christy Mahon. She wonders, indeed, whether her lover may not have more than one string to his bow. In order to ascertain this important fact she makes use of typically feminine wiles. When Christy proposes to her, she answers: "You've right daring to go ask me that, when all knows you'll be starting to some girl in your own townland, when your father's rotten in four months, or five."[3] She gains her object without delay. Christy becomes still more eager to win "the crowning prize," as he himself calls Pegeen.

The methods used by both girls to prompt their partners to action are practically identical. Hilde's use of the seemingly artless question whether *"my* master builder *dares* not—*cannot*—climb as high as he builds" in order to make the ageing Solness overtax his strength of mind and body, has already been commented upon.

Christy is "managed" by Pegeen after the same fashion. His decision to take part in the athletic contest, as a result of which he becomes the hero of the day, is made in response to Pegeen's invitation: "Pegeen says you're to come."[4] He cannot resist the temptation to join her: "I will then if Pegeen's beyond."

Thus both Hilde and Pegeen urge their heroes on to the point of either figurative or actual collapse. Faced by disaster, these women's unsatiable egotism reveals itself. Hilde's almost maniacal cry *"My—my* Master Builder!"[5] when Solness' death puts her scheming to an abrupt end, is echoed exactly in Pegeen's "wild lamentations:" "Oh, my grief, I've lost him surely. I've lost the

---

[1] *The Master Builder*, Act II, p. 317. Compare the passage in *The Lady from the Sea*, where Hilde's love of sensation is hinted at in her confession that she finds it "so thrilling to think of" the fact that the young artist who is stricken by a mortal disease "won't live long enough." (Act II, p. 216.)

[2] *Ibid.*, Act II, p. 303.

[3] *The Playboy of the Western World*, Act III, pp. 89-90.

[4] *Ibid.*, Act II, p. 74.

[5] *The Master Builder*, Act III, p. 365.

only Playboy of the Western World."[1] This is, it seems to me, in all probability the most literal example of Ibsenian influence in the works of Synge.

The comparison between Hilde and Pegeen may consequently be said to show that both are representative specimens of the high-strung, hysterical type of girl, always seeking for some new sensation. Hilde's "frightfully thrilling" is a typical expression of this attitude towards life.

Finally, it may be of interest to note that Synge, like Ibsen, succeeds in making his extraordinary heroine an interesting and strangely fascinating if not exactly a sympathetic character. Bernard Shaw, in his book *The Quintessence of Ibsenism*, does not hesitate to say: "Hilda Wangel, who kills the Master Builder literally to amuse herself, is the most fascinating of sympathetic girl-heroines."[2]

Consequently, still another connecting link between Ibsen and Synge is found in the fact that neither of them leaves his heroine to the tender mercies of the audience. Solness, like Hilde Wangel, tried to achieve "the impossible." So did Christy and Pegeen. *"L'amour de l'impossible"* proves fatal to both couples.

---

[1] *The Playboy of the Western World*, Act III, p. 113.

[2] Bernard Shaw, *The Quintessence of Ibsenism. Now Completed to the Death of Ibsen* (London 1913), p. 161.

CHAPTER VI

Deirdre of the Sorrows

Love's Comedy

Synge's last drama, *Deirdre of the Sorrows*, posthumously published in 1910, represents in many ways a turning-point in the author's career. To begin with, the very subject seems to imply that Synge had begun to weary of the peasant drama. In any case, *Deirdre of the Sorrows* must be regarded as a conscious effort on the part of Synge to remodel his style and add to the scope of his drama. "Folk tragedy," Boyd remarks, "even though the fable be classic, is the only term which accurately describes Synge's *Deirdre*, which is, therefore, an essential part of the author's work, not an exceptional experiment, as some have maintained."[1]

Another characteristic of this drama, as compared with the earlier ones, is its autobiographical tendency. The fact that Synge was a dying man when he wrote *Deirdre* no doubt explains the note of intensity found both in the dialogue and the inner psychology of the play. Furthermore, one is struck with the dignity, that characterizes the part of Deirdre. "She had the power to lure to reverence even Synge, who could be very scornful of dead queens."[2]

*

Synge's tragedy shows us Deirdre as the ward of Conchubor who intends to marry her when she comes of age, although he has been warned that the girl will bring disaster to his throne. But the old king's plans are thwarted by Deirdre and her lover Naisi

---

[1] Boyd, *The Contemporary Drama of Ireland*, p. 109.
[2] Francis Bickley, "*Deirdre*," *The Irish Review*, July 1912, p. 252.

who manage to escape to Scotland after being secretly married. Deirdre and Naisi live happily in the new country for seven years, until one day their lonely hiding-place is discovered by Conchubor's ambassador. He offers them the king's pardon and invites them to go back to the royal court. Both Deirdre and Naisi finally accept the offer and return to Ireland. Soon afterwards Naisi is slain by the treacherous king. Deirdre, unable to live on without her lover, dies by her own hand.

*

As regards Deirdre, we are faced with many interesting questions. To begin with, why does she want to escape with Naisi? No doubt because he is young and attractive and Conchubor a fierce old man. But that is only part of the answer. Naisi also appeals to her because he represents the spirit of revolt against the tyranny of the old king, embodying at the same time an adventurous and a glorious future. Another important question is this: Having found happiness in a foreign country, why does Deirdre want to go back to Ireland? Again the answer is a complicated one. One of her motives is no doubt that she cannot bear to live for ever in exile from her beloved country. Another reason is to be found in the fact that she has never been able to forget that her real name is Deirdre of the Sorrows. So in the end she experiences a certain ecstasy in facing her destiny. And yet Deirdre's decision to return home is primarily due to a change in the relations between her and Naisi. The very day the king's pardon was offered to them she overhears part of her husband's conversation with the ambassador, revealing Naisi's fear that his love for Deirdre may not last for ever. And so Deirdre, fearing the loss of Naisi's love and the passing of youth and beauty, has no other choice but to return to Ireland. Only by seeking a premature death can she conquer time and immortalize her love.

Thus the theme of renunciation is of primary importance in the interplay of varying motives which presages Deirdre's final step. Now, it so happens that this very theme is also to some extent a *Leitmotif* in the works of Ibsen. We hit upon it for the first time in some of the author's early lyrics, *e.g. The Fiddlers (Spillemænd)* and the long poem *On the Vidda (På vidderne)*, written in 1859–60.

Love's Comedy (1862) is about the first of Ibsen's plays to present the same theme of sacrifice and renunciation which is then repeated in *Brand, The Master Builder, Little Eyolf, John Gabriel Borkman,* and *When We Dead Awaken,* Ibsen's *Dramatic Epilogue.*

For our purpose it is perhaps sufficient to consider *Love's Comedy* as all the other plays are merely variations of the same theme.

*

In Falk and Svanhild Ibsen presents a young couple who revolt against the meanness and pettiness of ordinary people. He is a poet seeking inspiration in his love for Svanhild. She is to help him in his struggle against the conventions of society and lend significance to his literary career. At first, the young iconoclast delights in the riot he creates by his radical attacks upon wedded love. But soon Falk and Svanhild begin to doubt the lasting quality of their own feelings. And so, as neither of them can bear that their passion should fade, they agree to separate while their love is still triumphant.

*

As will be seen from this brief summary, there is a curious resemblance of subject between *Love's Comedy* and *Deirdre.* Both treat of a love that demands all or nothing. There is also the same fear of the decay of love. Finally, both Svanhild and Deirdre prefer to anticipate events. Voluntary renunciation makes it possible for both to secure eternal love. Thus Deirdre might well have joined in Svanhild's exultant cry:

> Now for this earthly life I have foregone thee,—
> But for the life eternal I have won thee![1]

Finally, the following couplets from *Love's Comedy* seem to offer another interesting parallel to the situation in *Deirdre.*[2]

> SVANHILD. No, no, not thus our day of bliss shall wane,
> Flag drearily to west in clouds and rain;—
> But at high noontide, when it is most bright,
> Plunge sudden, like a meteor, into night!
> FALK [*in anguish*]. What would you, Svanhild?

---

[1] *Love's Comedy,* Act III (C. W., vol. I, p. 451).

[2] Cf. Bradbrook, *op. cit.,* p. 37, note 2.

SVANHILD.   We are of the Spring;
No Autumn shall come after, when the bird
Of music in thy breast shall not be heard,
And long not thither where it first took wing.
Nor ever Winter shall his snowy shroud
Lay on the clay-cold body of our bliss;—
This Love of ours, ardent and glad and proud,
Pure of disease's taint and age's cloud,
Shall die the young and glorious thing it is!

— — —

FALK. O, I divine thee! But—to sever thus!
Now, when the portals of the world stand wide,—
When the blue spring is bending over us,
On the same day that plighted thee my bride!
SVANHILD. Just therefore must we part. Our joy's torch fire
Will from this moment wane till it expire![1]

Turning to Synge, this is how his Deirdre bids farewell to her love:

It's this hour we're between the daytime and a night where there is sleep for ever, and isn't it a better thing to be following on to a near death, than to be bending the head down, and dragging with the feet, and seeing one day a blight showing upon love where it is sweet and tender?

— — —

There are as many ways to wither love as there are stars in a night of Samhain; but there is no way to keep life, or love with it, a short space only . . .[2]

— — —

It is not a small thing to be rid of grey hairs, and the loosening of the teeth. (*With a sort of triumph.*) It was the choice of lives we had in the clear woods, and in the grave we're safe, surely. . . .[3]

Summing up, we should like to say that the principal source of *Deirdre* is undoubtedly the autobiographical element already referred to. The author's own tragic situation no doubt accounts for the remarkable intensity which characterizes his handling of the Deirdre-*motif*. Synge wrote his last drama literally on his deathbed. He knew that the call had come. But he did not tell

---

[1] *Love's Comedy*, Act III, pp. 448–450.
[2] *Deirdre of the Sorrows*, Act II, pp. 162–163.
[3] *Ibid.*, Act III, p. 195.

anybody, except his betrothed, Maire O'Neill, the talented actress whose name is closely associated with outstanding performances of his plays.

In pointing out the above parallels, our sole object has been to draw attention to another source that might possibly have inspired certain aspects of Synge's drama.

CHAPTER VII

Notes on the Dialogue of Ibsen and Synge

Before leaving the subject of Synge's indebtedness to Ibsen, a few words must be added about the treatment of dialogue in the works of the two dramatists. For there is much in favour of the view that Synge's method of utilizing dialogue as a means of characterization can be traced back to Ibsen.

The latter's remarkable feeling for the basic importance of language as a means of character drawing has often been overlooked or even questioned, both by Scandinavian and foreign critics. To some extent this is undoubtedly due to inadequate translations. Even the standard translation made by William Archer, though I have used it for this study, in my opinion can hardly be considered an adequate means of showing us Ibsen as a great master of language. Though fairly true to the original, and a great achievement as such, Archer's translation is often rather mechanical as well as lacking both in form and spirit.

Dr. Tennant, when dealing with the question of Ibsen's style, passes the following verdict which seems to me to result from his having relied too closely upon inferior renderings of the original.

"Ibsen's treatment of prose dialogue, though conversational, is strikingly lacking in variation. Nearly all of his characters speak the same language, and Hjalmar Ekdal is one of the few whom he succeeds in characterizing by individual turns of speech."[1]

This is definitely a premature conclusion. For even if we confine ourselves to those of Ibsen's plays which have been discussed in this study, we hit upon no two characters expressing themselves

---

[1] Tennant, *op. cit.*, pp. 119–120.

in the same idiom. Take for instance the opening act of *The League of Youth* where the different persons are clearly defined and individualized by means of the very first sentences they utter. Or we may listen to the dialogue in *Ghosts* for other examples of the playwright's skilful use of individual idiom as an indication of character. Indeed, we know that Ibsen told his Swedish translator of *Ghosts* to pay special attention to the dialogue. For no single character, he said, expresses himself in exactly the same way as another.[1] That this is so, is evident from *The Master Builder* which offers one of the best examples of Ibsen's unique treatment of dialogue, as has been pointed out by Miss Bradbrook:

"In this play Ibsen succeeds in doing what few dramatists except Shakespeare can do; each character has his own idiom, his own particular accent, so that the whole dialogue is impregnated with direct dramatic significance. — — — Solness's character is given in his speech, in his growls and hasty oaths, his vehement outbursts, his pounces of irascibility, which render directly his passionate struggle for life against the creeping paralysis of fear and remorse that is seizing him. Hilde's usual speech is an excited and slangy gallop: her characteristic cry is 'Straks!' — 'Now this minute!' but her vivid changes of mood are reflected in sudden metaphors — 'our cloud-castle ...' 'I have come out of a grave ...' Aline's pitiful clipped brevities, her parrot-like repetition of 'It is my duty,' would become monotonous if her part were longer."[2]

In this way we find that Ibsen was always most anxious to reproduce the individual accents of his characters. This holds true not only of Ibsen's great psychological studies; it is equally characteristic of the professional types which figure in his plays. Mrs. Alving in *Ghosts* has to put up with Pastor Manders' clerical jargon; Rosmer in *Rosmersholm* must listen to the stilted official language of his brother-in-law, the headmaster, and so on. In short, Ibsen's achievement represents nothing less than a revolutionary development in the drama of Norwegian, and therefore European prose dialogue.

*

Turning from Ibsen to Synge, it is not without interest to notice that his reputation as a great master of dramatic dialogue has

---

[1] Lamm, *op. cit.*, p. 143.
[2] Bradbrook, *op. cit.*, pp. 126–127.

been open to a similar discussion ever since his plays first startled the world. While some critics do not hesitate to compare Synge to Shakespeare in this respect, there are others who deliberately underestimate his true genius for dialogue.

It is a significant fact that only last year an attack upon Synge in general and his idiom in particular was published in his own country. A young Irish critic, Mr. Owen Quinn, was bold enough to set forth that "the language suffers from a defect it has in common with the language of decadent Elizabethan drama, the drama of Beaumont and Fletcher—too much tongue, insufficient thought." The critic goes on to speak of Synge's "mental flaccidity that gave rise to the dialogue," the "quaintness" of which, we are told, "is saved from being ridiculous only by the quaintness of his characters."[1]

In spite of his efforts the critic fails, however, to convince the reader of the validity of his highly subjective opinions. For there are no "quaint characters" in *Riders to the Sea*—a fact which even Mr. Quinn admits—and hardly any in *Deirdre*—to mention only the most obvious exceptions. As for the statement that "mental flaccidity—gave rise to the dialogue" in Synge's plays, this is unjust not only to the playwright himself, but to the entire population of the Irish countryside. For we have Synge's own words for the fact that "in writing *The Playboy of the Western World*, as in my other plays, I have used one or two words only that I have not heard among the country people of Ireland — — —." "Anyone," he adds, "who has lived in real intimacy with the Irish peasantry will know that the wildest sayings and ideas in this play are tame indeed, compared with the fancies one may hear in any little hillside cabin in Geesala, or Carraroe, or Dingle Bay."[2]

Synge's plays, it is true, are all written in Anglo-Irish, a dialect influenced by the Gaelic idiom. But within that dialect, what a differentiation of language! There are no two characters who speak alike. Synge has endowed them all with a highly individualized accent so that each figure stands out clearly from the others in the same play.

---

[1] Owen Quinn, "*No Garland for John Synge*," *Envoy*, October 1950, p. 50.
[2] *Preface* to *The Playboy of the Western World*.

Apart from obvious reminiscences of the Bible *e.g.* the Psalms, as well as of the Elizabethan drama, Synge's treatment of the language and more particularly his way of individualization by means of the dialogue in many ways remind us of Ibsen. Synge, it will be remembered, writing in Anglo-Irish, "that passionate mixture of Irish and English,"[1] spoke scornfully of "the joyless and pallid words" of the Norwegian playwright but nevertheless it seems to me that he fell under the spell of *Peer Gynt*, the poetic ecstasy of which is echoed in *The Playboy*.

Even a cursory survey of Synge's plays reveals his extraordinary gift of individualizing his characters by means of their idiom. In his early play *In the Shadow of the Glen* we come across the vivid portrait of Nora Burke who is caught in her own trap as the glen turns out to be a blind alley:

"I do be thinking in the long nights it was a big fool I was that time, Michael Dara; for what good is a bit of a farm with cows on it, and sheep on the back hills, when you do be sitting looking out from a door the like of that door, and seeing nothing but the mists rolling down the bog, and the mists again and they rolling up the bog, and hearing nothing but the wind crying out in the bits of broken trees were left from the great storm, and the streams roaring with the rain."[2]

Riders to the Sea deals with the tragic conflict between the old generation and the young in their relations to the sea. Maurya's pessimistic question: "Isn't it a hard and cruel man won't hear a word from an old woman, and she holding him from the sea?" is overruled by the optimism of her daughter Cathleen: "It's the life of a young man to be going on the sea, and who would listen to an old woman with one thing and she saying it over?"[3] Finally, when the sea has robbed Maurya of her only remaining son, the old woman's empty loneliness is mirrored in words which also reveal her peaceful resignation:

"They're all gone now, and there isn't anything more the sea can do to me ... I'll have no call now to be up crying and praying when the wind breaks from the south, and you can hear the surf is in the

---

[1] A. G. van Hamel, "*On Anglo-Irish Syntax*," *Englische Studien* XLV (1912), p. 274.

[2] *In the Shadow of the Glen*, p. 19.

[3] *Riders to the Sea*, p. 37.

east, and the surf is in the west, making a great stir with the two noises, and they hitting one on the other. I'll have no call now to be going down and getting Holy Water in the dark nights after Samhain, and I won't care what way the sea is when the other women will be keening."[1]

And the play ends with Maurya submitting herself to the decrees of Providence: "No man at all can be living for ever, and we must be satisfied."[2]

The figure of Maurya gains in stature mainly by means of such unforgettable turns of speech as the last-quoted phrase. Indeed, Synge's vision of the poor old fisherwoman is one of the best examples of how the dramatist's command of language expressing his intimate knowledge of the human heart enabled him to create a portrait that must also rank as an interesting psychological study.

In this context it is not without interest to recall the fact that Ibsen with a similar intention to reveal his characters by means of their idiom, managed to put life into the portrait of the otherwise somewhat petrified Mrs. Solness in *The Master Builder*. The pathetic little phrases put into her mouth by the author individualize Solness' wife so that finally she becomes a touching figure in her tragic resignation. Thus her robot-like management of the house, together with her constant harping on the subject of the dolls, which figure in her morbid imagination as substitutes for her dead children, stress the poignancy of her mourning.

In *The Tinker's Wedding* we hit upon one of Synge's most primitive characters in the figure of old Mary Byrne who is blessed with an unquenchable thirst (which keeps not only herself but the whole play going). Left by her son and his doxy, she sums up her situation in a fine speech which gives her away completely:

"What good am I this night, God help me? What good are the grand stories I have when it's few would listen to an old woman, few but a girl maybe would be in great fear the time her hour was come, or a little child wouldn't be sleeping with the hunger on a cold night? — — — Maybe the two of them have a good right to be walking out the little short while they'd be young; but if they have itself, they'll not keep Mary Byrne from her full pint when the night's fine, and there's a dry moon in the sky. — — — Jemmy Neill's a decent lad; and

---

[1] *Riders to the Sea*, p. 49.
[2] *Ibid.*, p. 52.

he'll give me a good drop for the can; and maybe if I keep near the
peelers to-morrow for the first bit of the fair, herself won't strike me
at all; and if she does itself, what's a little stroke on your head beside
sitting lonesome on a fine night, hearing the dogs barking, and the
bats squeeking, and you saying over, it's a short while only till you
die."[1]

As for the young tinkers, Michael Byrne and Sarah Casey, they
are admirably portrayed in the opening scene of the play which
reveals the true nature of their strange love-affair as well as their
different attitude towards each other.

In *The Well of the Saints* the beautiful dream-world of the blind
couple offers an effective contrast with the prosaic outlook of their
fellow countrymen. The dialogue of Martin and Mary Doul faith-
fully mirrors their incurable escapism, reaching its climax in the
old man's final attack upon the saint and the world of the seeing:

> "For if it's a right some of you have to be working and sweating the
> like of Timmy the smith, and a right some of you have to be fasting
> and praying and talking holy talk the like of yourself, I'm thinking
> it's a good right ourselves have to be sitting blind, hearing a soft
> wind turning round the little leaves of the spring and feeling the sun,
> and we not tormenting our souls with the sight of the gray days, and
> the holy men, and the dirty feet is trampling the world."[2]

Turning to *The Playboy of the Western World*, we find a richly
developed dialogue which shows us Synge's power of individualization reaching its perfection.

Pegeen's father, the easy-going publican, neglects his daughter
in order to satisfy his own alcoholic cravings at the wake of Kate
Cassidy. The random speech of this buoyant character reveals
the fact that he is in the habit of retreating into an alcoholic haze
which gives a free rein to his wilful daughter.

Pegeen's admirer, the chicken-hearted Shawn Keogh, avoids
the temptations of the flesh for fear of Father Reilly and "the Holy
Father and the Cardinals of Rome." Furthermore there is the
merry widow who "has buried her children and destroyed her man."
Actuated by avarice she scurries through the play in search of a
new bargain.

---

[1] *The Tinker's Wedding*, Act I, pp. 156–157.
[2] *The Well of the Saints*, Act III, p. 130.

As for the young couple, Pegeen and Christy Mahon, some of their most significant remarks have already been quoted above, such as the girl's genuine surprise at the change that has happened to her: "And to think it's me is talking sweetly, Christy Mahon, and I the fright of seven townlands for my biting tongue. Well, the heart's a wonder — — —."[1] The boy's conceited arrogance when he finds himself master of the situation is no less characteristic of his chameleon-like accomodation to circumstances:

> "Well, it's a clean bed and soft with it, and it's great luck and company I've won me in the end of time—two fine women fighting for the likes of me—till I'm thinking this night wasn't I a foolish fellow not to kill my father in the years gone by."[2]

Similarly the love dialogue between Christy and Pegeen may be said to mirror their different characters as well as their aims and ambitions. Though already commented upon, the following apposite remark on their grandiloquent discourse might be added. In his essay on "*The Art of Conversation*" De Selincourt writes:

> "In Synge's dialogue you will notice just those qualities that make the essence of all good talk—the play of fancy in each speaker, and the manner in which each catches up the words of the other, developing his points, and egging him on to still higher flights of eloquence."[3]

This is equally applicable to Ibsen's dialogue at its best. We need only mention *Peer Gynt* or Hilde Wangel and the Master Builder.

Though Synge had to leave his last play unfinished, the conversation of *Deirdre* is nevertheless remarkably rich and varied. The ruthlessness of Conchubor towards Deirdre — "It's little I heed for what she was born; she'll be my comrade surely." —[4] is toned down and explained by the old king's pathetic loneliness:

> "There's one sorrow has no end surely—that's being old and lonesome. — — — But you and I will have a little peace in Emain, with harps playing, and old men telling stories at the fall of night."[5]

---

[1] *The Playboy of the Western World*, Act III, p. 93.

[2] *Ibid.*, Act I, p. 41.

[3] Ernest De Selincourt, *Wordsworthian and Other Studies* (Oxford 1947), pp. 199-200.

[4] *Deirdre of the Sorrows*, Act I, p. 122.

[5] *Ibid.*, Act III, p. 187.

The heart and mind of Lavarcham, Deirdre's faithful old servant, are set on thwarting the evil intentions of gods and men towards her nursling. Once her suspicions have been aroused she does not shrink from incurring the wrath of the High King: "it wasn't for your like she was born at all."[1] Out of the same motive, Lavarcham is sometimes capable of opposing Deirdre herself in terms which reveal the savage directness of her mind:

DEIRDRE (a little haughtily). Let you not raise your voice against me, Lavarcham, if you have will itself to guard Naisi.
LAVARCHAM (breaking out in anger). Naisi is it? I didn't care if the crows were stripping his thigh-bones at the dawn of day. It's to stop your own despair and wailing, and you waking up in a cold bed, without the man you have your heart on, I am raging now."[2]

Conchubor's spy, Owen, has no doubt borrowed many traits from the fool of the Elizabethan drama. Accordingly he is used by Synge mainly for the sake of contrast. Owen's character is skilfully summed up in his wreckless passion for Deirdre, a passion which forms the background to his cynical revelations as to the future of Deirdre and her lover Naisi.

"Well, go, take your choice. Stay here and rot with Naisi or go to Conchubor in Emain. Conchubor's wrinkled fool with a swelling belly on him, and eyes falling downward from his shining crown; Naisi should be stale and weary. Yet there are many roads, Deirdre, and I tell you I'd liefer be bleaching in a bog-hole than living on without a touch of kindness from your eyes and voice. It's a poor thing to be so lonesome you'd squeeze kisses on a cur dog's nose."[3]

Of the two lovers, Naisi is rather colourless compared to the vivid portrait of Deirdre. His naive optimism meets with Deirdre's dispassionate judgement:

NAISI. I've said we'd stay in Alban always.
DEIRDRE. There's no place to stay always.[4]

— — —

NAISI. — — — it's right to be away from all people when two lovers have their love only. Come away and we'll be safe always.

1 Deirdre of the Sorrows, Act I, p. 122.
2 Ibid., Act, II, p. 149.
3 Ibid., Act II, pp. 153–154.
4 Ibid., Act II, p. 161.

DEIRDRE (*broken-hearted*). There is no safe place, Naisi, on the ridge of the world.[1]

— — —

NAISI. — — — Come away into the safety of the woods.

DEIRDRE (*shaking her head slowly*). There are as many ways to wither love as there are stars in a night of Samhain; but there is no way to keep life, or love with it, a short space only . . .[2]

The disillusioned attitude of Deirdre is quite in keeping with her pessimistic view as to the instability of love and of earthly happiness. Deirdre's fear of getting old and of losing her lover help to bring about her tragic end. But in seeking a premature death rather than waiting for her declining age, she dies triumphant, facing in the right direction:

"— — — isn't it a better thing to be following on to a near death, than to be bending the head down, and dragging with the feet, and seing one day a blight showing upon love where it is sweet and tender?"[3]

— — —

"I have put away sorrow like a shoe that is worn out and muddy, for it is I have had a life that will be envied by great companies. It was not by a low birth I made kings uneasy, and they sitting in the halls of Emain. It was not a low thing to be chosen by Conchubor, who was wise, and Naisi had no match for bravery. It is not a small thing to be rid of grey hairs, and the loosening of the teeth. (*With a sort of triumph.*) It was the choice of lives we had in the clear woods, and in the grave we're safe, surely . . ."[4]

*

Thus we have found that both Ibsen and Synge are alike in their effort at individualizing the figures of their plays by means of their own speech. The result is a direct form of characterization where different idioms are used as an indication of different characters.

Ibsen is an acknowledged master of the retrospective technique. The antecedents of his characters are gradually revealed by means of their own remarks which may seem harmless and casual enough when they are made, only to be brought to bear on the past with almost uncanny power in the *dénouement* of the plays.

---

[1] *Deirdre of the Sorrows*, Act II, p. 162.
[2] *Ibid.*, Act II, p. 163.
[3] *Ibid.*, Act II, pp. 162–163.
[4] *Ibid.*, Act III, p. 195.

When we have noticed to what highly impressive use Ibsen put this retrospective technique, it is only natural for us to find that Synge should have adopted and developed it for his own purpose.

The Norwegian master is known to have aimed at dramatic concentration and elimination as regards both the action and the number of his characters, the result of which tendency is clearly manifested in his later works.

Similarly, Synge's method of composition is that of Ibsen. Like his forerunner, he first observed and made a great number of notes. Then, having selected and concentrated his stuff, he settled down to remodel it with unerring craftsmanship.

The one-act play of Synge represents a daring exploitation as well as a remarkable development of Ibsen's technique. In a comment upon *In the Shadow of the Glen,* Howe maintains that "outside Ibsen, perhaps we may say outside Rosmersholm, there is no match for the way in which the past is summarised for us while a group of people move and speak, with a perfectly natural regard for present truth, before our eyes."[1] "And Synge," he adds, "unlike Ibsen in Rosmersholm, has only a few lines, and not four acts, in which to resume their past. Every line, therefore, must speak of their past, must reveal their character in the present, and must point us forward; and all this with perfect deference to reality."[2]

To have brought the retrospective technique to a height of perfection that not even Ibsen would ever have dreamt of, will be to Synge's lasting credit.

---

[1] Howe, *op. cit.,* p. 48.

[2] *Ibid.,* pp. 48–49.

CHAPTER VIII

Synge and the Problem Play

The above analysis of Synge's plays and some of Ibsen's has revealed not only obvious similarities but also some fundamental differences as regards ideas, milieu and tendency. It is quite clear that Synge, unlike Ibsen in his capacity of preacher and moralist, takes great pains not to commit himself as to what is right or wrong in a given dramatic situation. Such questions he obviously considers to be something of a side issue. Consequently, we are now in a position to discuss Synge's plays under a different, yet closely related aspect, indicated in the heading of this chapter.

The previous investigation has shown that there are many connecting links between the drama of Ibsen and that of Synge as far as subject, character drawing and technique are concerned. But so far the discussion has not taken into account the important question raised above, *i.e.* whether Synge actually intended to raise and discuss problems in his plays, in the manner of his Norwegian predecessor.

Let us begin with a preliminary statement on Ibsen the reformer. It has long been customary to stress his qualities as a thinker and a social critic at the expense of his great achievement as a poet. Now, according to many recent critics Ibsen's "thinking" is but rarely on a level with his poetical inspiration. In other words, Ibsen is always in the first place a great poet and artist. The best proof of this fact is that so many of his problem plays have kept the stage long after the burning questions they discuss have ceased to stir our imagination.

Synge, as we saw above, emphasized the didactic element in Ibsen's plays and in consequence deliberately underestimated the poetic genius of his Norwegian forerunner. Unquestionably, the didactic element in Ibsen is far from negligible. But the "lesson" is usually most skilfully wrapped up in the poetical inventions of the creative artist. Thus Synge's chief objection to Ibsen that "the drama, like the symphony, does not teach or prove anything," only covers part of Ibsen's achievement. As an artist, the latter was very well aware of the qualities and possibilities of his own drama when he made his famous statement: "I prefer to ask, it is not my task to answer."

When, in this way, we have tried to establish more accurate proportions between Ibsen the poet and Ibsen the preacher, we are free to examine the different way in which he and Synge approach their subjects.

A survey of Ibsen's plays shows that he directs his attention to a great variety of problems. He was a keen observer of human conflicts rather than of actual life. For it is one of his characteristics that his thinking, always ahead of his personal experience, opened up vistas of life unknown to the lonely man himself. Thus *A Doll's House* deals with the emancipation of women, *Ghosts* discusses society and heredity, *An Enemy of the People* analyses the conflict between extreme individualism and the morals of the masses, *The Wild Duck* exposes the "life-lie," and so on. The problem tendency is unmistakable throughout the majority of Ibsen's plays. Behind them all there is much thinking and planning. But only through the far more important poetical process initiated by the artist himself do they crystallize into works of great literary distinction.

*

If, now, we turn to Synge, adopting the same point of view, we are at once struck by the non-didactic tenor of his drama. This is quite in keeping with Synge's literary creed as it found expression in the prefaces to his plays. The present study has so far referred to Synge as a critic only in general terms. In consequence, it remains to make clear in some detail his attitude towards the problem play. The fact that Synge is at great pains to emphasize his conviction that the drama should not teach or prove anything, does not, of course, indicate the absence of problems from the drama he advocates. Nor is his claim for "joy" and "humour" incompatible with the problem play as such. In my opinion, however, it offers the logical starting-point for a true insight into the significance he ascribes to the problems which figure in his own plays.

The previous study has drawn attention to the close conformity of the main subjects of Synge's plays to some of the *motifs* generally associated with Ibsen. But a further analysis reveals another interesting fact about the two authors. With Ibsen there is as a rule an unmistakable correlation between the problem itself and the persons who are faced with it; the two balance and emphasize each other. In Synge's case, on the other hand, the problem forms no such integral part of the main plot. For unlike Ibsen, Synge is first and foremost an observer of the events of life, rather than of inner conflicts. In my opinion, problems as such are devoid of interest to him. "In these days," he writes in the introduction to *The Tinker's Wedding*, "the playhouse is too often stocked with the drugs of many seedy problems."

Nevertheless, a problem is inherent in practically all of Synge's plays. *In the Shadow of the Glen* depicts the conflicts of married life, as well as the development of character; *Riders to the Sea* deals with the fateful fascination of elemental forces in life; *The Well of the Saints* shows us the struggle between reality and illusion, and so on. But unlike *The Doll's House*, *The Lady from the Sea* and *The Wild Duck*, where these problems are carefully examined and interpreted, Synge's plays offer no such analysis. With him life's conflicts have a value in themselves and therefore there is no need for additional moralizing. Unlike Ibsen, who used to puzzle his audience and to disturb their peace of mind, Synge expressly disclaims any similar intention. There is, as stated above, hardly any tendency behind his dramas. But when he chose to dabble in literary criticism, *e.g.* when writing prefaces to his plays, the purpose is clear enough. For there can be no doubt that he wrote his introductions with a view to defending his own drama against rival schools both at home and abroad.[1]

In view of what has been stated above, it seems to me that we are safe in saying: Synge's attitude towards the problem play tends

---

[1] Cf. *Introduction*, p. 13.

to show that he did not want to increase the number of such plays
if he could help it. Or as a critic puts it:

"He does not intellectualize the drama, he does not want to con-
struct and interpret events, he gathers scraps of actual life and lets
them carry their own meaning. That this meaning occasionally becomes
a very deep one as in the *Well of the Saints* is in the subject, not in the
author's brain. There is nothing more alien to Synge's mind than problem plays. His is a poetic vision of life but of existing, actual life."[1]

---

[1] Liljegren in *Englische Studien* LVIII (1924), pp. 295-296.

Conclusion

The present analysis seems to me to warrant the conclusion that there is an undeniable affinity between Ibsen's dramas and those of Synge, plainly indicated in the points of resemblance cited above. The Ibsenian trends in Synge's plays are indeed so many and so heterogeneous that, in my opinion, they must be regarded as evidence of ubiquitous influence exercised upon him by the Norwegian dramatist. The juxtaposition of Synge's plays with those of Ibsen seems to reveal an indubitable correlation of theme, character drawing, setting and technique.

This similarity, however, does not in any way detract from the literary distinction of the Irish playwright. The proof of Synge's originality lies in the fact that the Ibsenian influence was never permitted to efface the genuine Irishness of his literary profile. That this is so, is best shown by the fact that so many scholars have been able to read Synge without observing his indebtedness to Ibsen.

Synge's criticism of Ibsen's drama, however, makes it possible for the reader to discover the main points of divergence between the two dramatists, showing how Synge with his insistence on "joy" and "humour" finds matter for a completely amoral comedy, or tragi-comedy, in a subject already treated by Ibsen, the ethicist and moralist, as a tragedy. But the negative attitude displayed by Synge towards Ibsen can no longer conceal the fact that, like the Norwegian dramatist, he, too, moves within the sphere of problem plays. If the Norwegian is a writer of problem plays, the Irishman is a writer of plays with problems in them.

The parallels drawn between Ibsen and Synge have made it possible to ascertain that, generally speaking, the Irish playwright may be said to take interest in situations that involve the same questions as those dealt with by his Norwegian forerunner. He also maps out these problems in much the same way, and the conclusions, if any, are those already arrived at by Ibsen.

Thus Synge himself bears ample witness to the validity of his own artistic creed, as expressed in the preface to *The Playboy:* "All art is a collaboration."

Bibliography

A.

IBSEN, HENRIK, *Collected Works*. Entirely revised and edited by William Archer. Vols. I–XI. (Heinemann, London 1906–1908).

Some of Ibsen's plays appeared almost simultaneously in Norway and in England. Most of his dramas were accessible to English readers in a uniform edition, published during the 1890's. Ibsen's last play, *When We Dead Awaken* (1899), was translated into English as early as 1900.

SYNGE, JOHN MILLINGTON, *Four Plays*. (Maunsel & Company, Dublin 1911).

——, *Two Plays*. (Maunsel & Company, Dublin 1911).

——, *Poems and Translations*. (Maunsel & Company, Dublin 1911).

——,. *In Wicklow, West Kerry and Connemara*. (Maunsel & Company, Dublin 1911).

——, *The Aran Islands*. (Maunsel & Company, Dublin 1912).

B.

ARCHER WILLIAM, *The Old Drama and the New. An Essay in Re-Valuation*. (London 1923).

AUFHAUSER, A., *Sind die Dramen von John Millington Synge durch französische Vorbilder beeinflusst?* (Munich 1935).

BICKLEY, FRANCIS, *J. M. Synge and the Irish Dramatic Movement*. (London 1912).

——, "Deirdre," *The Irish Review*, July 1912.

BIENS, FRIEDRICH, *A. E., George W. Russell. Sein Leben und Werk im Lichte seiner theosophischen Weltanschauung*. (Greifswald 1934).

BJERSBY, BIRGIT, *The Interpretation of the Cuchulain Legend in the Works of W. B. Yeats*. (Diss., Uppsala 1950).

BOURGEOIS, MAURICE, *John Millington Synge and the Irish Theatre*. (London 1913). With extensive bibliography.

BOYD, ERNEST A., *Ireland's Literary Renaissance*. (Dublin & London 1916).

——, *The Contemporary Drama of Ireland*. (Dublin & London 1918).

——, "The Abbey Theatre," *The Irish Review*, February 1913.

BRADBROOK, M. C., *Ibsen the Norwegian. A Revaluation*. (London 1946).

BRYANT, SOPHIE, *The Genius of the Gael. A Study in Celtic Psychology and its Manifestations*. (London 1913). With a chapter on *The Gael in Literature*.

BULL, FRANCIS, *Henrik Ibsens Peer Gynt*. (Oslo 1947).

Byrne, Dawson, *The Story of Ireland's National Theatre*. (Dublin 1929).

Clarke, Austin, *Poetry in Modern Ireland*. (Dublin 1951).

Corkery, Daniel, *Synge and Anglo-Irish Literature*. (Oxford 1931, 1947).

Downs, Brian W., *Ibsen. The Intellectual Background*. (Cambridge 1946).

——, *A Study of Six Plays by Ibsen*. (Cambridge 1950).

Eliot, T. S., *Elizabethan Essays*. (London 1934, 1942).

Estill, Adelaide Duncan, *The Sources of Synge*. (Diss., Philadelphia 1939).

Fehr, Bernhard, *Die englische Literatur des 19. und 20. Jahrhunderts*. Berlin 1923).

Gosse, Edmund W., *Ibsen*. (London 1907).

Gran, Gerhard, *Henrik Ibsen. Liv og verker*. I–II. (Kristiania 1918).

Greene, David H., "*The Shadow of the Glen and the Widow of Ephesus*," *PMLA* LXII (1947).

——, "*The Tinker's Wedding. A Revaluation*," *PMLA* LXII (1947).

Gwynn, Stephen, *Irish Literature and Drama*. (London 1936).

Hamel, A. G. van, "*On Anglo-Irish Syntax*," *Englische Studien* XLV (1912).

Henn, T. R., *The Lonely Tower. Studies in the Poetry of W. B. Yeats*. (London 1950). With a chapter on *Yeats and Synge*.

Hogan, J. J., *An Outline of English Philology. Chiefly for Irish Students*. (Dublin & Cork 1934). With a chapter on *The Grammar of Anglo-Irish*.

Howe, P. P., *J. M. Synge. A Critical Study*. (London 1912).

Huber, Robert, *Ibsens Bedeutung für das englische Drama*. (Diss., Marburg/L. 1914).

Ibsen, Bergliot, *De tre. Erindringer om Henrik Ibsen, Suzannah Ibsen, Sigurd Ibsen*. (Oslo 1948).

Jackson, Holbrook, *The Eighteen Nineties. A Review of Art and Ideas at the Close of the Nineteenth Century*. (London 1913).

Kehler, Henning, "*Studier i det Ibsenske Drama*," *Edda* IV–V (1915–1916).

Koht, Halvdan, *Henrik Ibsen. Eit diktarliv*. I–II. (Oslo 1928–1929).

Krieger, Hans, *John Millington Synge, ein dichter der 'keltischen renaissance'*. (Diss., Marburg/L. 1916).

Lamm, Martin, *Det moderna dramat*. (Stockholm 1948).

Legouis & Cazamian, *A History of English Literature*. (London 1943).

Mac Liammóir, Micheál, *Theatre in Ireland*. (Dublin 1950).

——, "*Problem Plays*," *The Irish Theatre*, edited by Lennox Robinson. (London 1939).

Maguire, Mary C., "*John Synge*," *The Irish Review*, March 1911.

Mair, G. H., *English Literature: Modern*. (London 1914).

Martyn, Edward, *The Heather Field* and *Maeve*. (London 1899). With an introduction by George Moore.

——, *An Enchanted Sea*. (London 1902).

——, *Grangecolman*. (Dublin 1912).

94

MASEFIELD, JOHN, *"John M. Synge," Recent Prose.* (London 1933).
MAYNE, RUTHERFORD, *The Drone and Other Plays.* (Dublin 1912).
MOORE, GEORGE, *'Hail and Farewell!' A Trilogy. Ave,* 1911; *Salve,* 1912; *Vale,* 1914. (London 1911—1914).
NICOLL, ALLARDYCE, *World Drama. From Aeschylus to Anouilh.* (London, Sidney 1949, 1951).
O'CONNOR, FRANK, *"Synge," The Irish Theatre,* edited by Lennox Robinson. (London 1939).
O'RIORDAN, CONAL, *"Synge in Dutch," The Irish Review,* December 1912.
QUINN, OWEN, *"No Garland for John Synge," Envoy,* October 1950.
QVAMME, BØRRE, *"Ibsen og det engelske Teater," Edda* XLII (1942).
RIVA, S., *La Tradizione Celtica e la Moderna Letteratura Irlandese: J. M. Synge.* (Rom 1937).
ROBINSON, LENNOX, *The Irish Theatre. Lectures delivered during the Abbey Theatre Festival in Dublin in August 1938.* Edited by Lennox Robinson. (London 1939).
RYDELL, GERDA, *Henrik Ibsen. En orientering i hans liv och diktning.* (Stockholm 1932).
SCHÜCK, HENRIK, *Illustrerad allmän litteraturhistoria.* I. (Stockholm 1919).
DE SELINCOURT, ERNEST, *Wordsworthian and Other Studies.* (Oxford 1947).
SHAW, BERNARD. *John Bull's Other Island.* (London 1907).
——, *The Quintessence of Ibsenism. Now Completed to the Death of Ibsen.* (London 1913).
STRONG, L. A. G., *"John Millington Synge," Bookman* (U. S. A.) LXXIII, April 1931.
SYNGE, S., *Letters to my Daughter.* Memories of John Millington Synge. (Dublin 1932).
TENNANT, P. F. D., *Ibsen's Dramatic Technique.* (Cambridge 1948).
THORNING, JUST, *J. M. Synge. En moderne irsk Dramatiker.* (Copenhagen 1921). Cf. S. B. Liljegren in *Englische Studien* LVIII (1924), pp. 294–296.
WIECZOREK, H., *Irische Lebenshaltung im neuen irischen Drama.* (Breslau 1937).
WILLIAMS, HAROLD, *Modern English Writers: Being a Study of Imaginative Literature 1890–1914.* (London 1918).
YEATS, WILLIAM BUTLER, *"J. M. Synge and the Ireland of his Time," Essays.* (London 1924).
——, *"Mr. Synge and his Plays."* Introduction to *The Well of the Saints.* (London 1905).
——, *"Preface to the First Edition of John M. Synge's Poems and Translations," Essays.* (London 1924).

Ibsen and the Beginnings of
Anglo-Irish Drama

II. Edward Martyn

EDWARD MARTYN
from the portrait by N. French McLachlan in the National
Gallery of Ireland.

Reproduced by courtesy of the National Gallery of Ireland.

UPSALA IRISH STUDIES

In Cooperation with J. CARNEY, J. J. HOGAN, *and* N. G. HOLMER

Edited by

S. B. LILJEGREN

V

Ibsen and the Beginnings of Anglo-Irish Drama

II. Edward Martyn

By

JAN SETTERQUIST

TO

MY MOTHER

Contents

8

Preface

My interest in Edward Martyn was aroused while I was still at work on the first part of the present study, dealing with Ibsen and J. M. Synge. I found that it was practically impossible to study any phase of the early history of the Irish Literary Renaissance without noticing the prominent position held by the author of *The Heather Field* and *Maeve*. A co-founder of the movement that subsequently led to the establishment of the Abbey Theatre, Edward Martyn spent much time and a considerable amount of money on the promotion of the fine arts, including music and the theatre.

Throughout his literary career the Irish dramatist acted as a living link between his own country and the Continent, seizing every opportunity to present foreign masterpieces upon the Irish stage, and urging his fellow-countrymen to study the works of Henrik Ibsen, whom he looked upon as the great innovator of the modern drama.

The immediate success of Martyn's first play, *The Heather Field*, with its Ibsenian group of characters, seemed to confirm his view that the Irish drama might be enriched from abroad. But before long he met with stubborn opposition from almost every quarter. With the passing of the years Martyn became an isolated man who had to cope with endless difficulties for carrying out his plans. Yet he refused to give in. Finally, towards the end of his life, he had the grim satisfaction of seeing the Abbey Theatre and the newly-formed Dublin Drama League engage upon the mutual task of staging the works of the famous continental playwrigths that he himself had tried to introduce some twenty years earlier.

By opposing the Yeatsian art shibboleth with its attack upon "the drama of Society", and by sponsoring Ibsen and the continental drama, Martyn secured a permanent place in the history of the Irish Dramatic Movement, a place he would never have occupied had he been content to dance attendance on Yeats and his followers.

Edward Martyn's indebtedness to Ibsen has been hinted at by many critics. But no attempt has as yet been made to give a full account of the close relationship that exists between the Irish dramatist and his Norwegian forerunner.

As in the case of J. M. Synge, I was put on the track by my teacher, Professor S. B. Liljegren, the pioneer in the field of Irish literary studies in this country. I am indebted to him for the subject of the present study which aroused my interest in the great writers of the Irish Literary Renaissance. I wish to express my deep gratitude to Professor Liljegren, not only for his generosity in allowing me to draw on the great resources of his scholarship, but also for the vivid interest he has taken in the progress of my work which owes so much to his encouragement and inspiration.

The aim of the present study is to give a detailed analysis of the various aspects, such as themes, character drawing and technique, that connect Martyn's plays with the Ibsenian theatre. In dealing with the subject I have selected those of the Irishman's published plays in which the foreign influence comes most clearly to the fore. This is the reason why I have chosen to neglect *The Dream Physician*, the action of which is as fantastic as its title. The whole play reads like a deliberate sneer at the lofty dreams and high-strung idealism of some of the author's earlier dramas. For the same reason I have also ignored two one-actors, *The Place-Hunters*, which is only a companion piece of *The Tale of a Town*, and *Romulus and Remus* which is, perhaps, best characterized by its sub-title "a symbolical extravaganza".

Several scholars have helped and encouraged me in the course of my researches. I am particularly indebted to Professor H. W. Donner under whose supervision this thesis was completed. I have benefited from his guidance in many ways and I am grateful to him for spending much time and wisdom on the manuscript of this book. I am also greatly in the debt of Professor Erik Tengstrand who kindly read an early version of some of my chapters and offered valuable suggestions. My sincere thanks are also directed to Professor J. J. Hogan who took an early interest in my studies and has continued to encourage me in many ways. I wish to pay a special tribute to Dr. Birgit Bramsbäck of the Department of English in Upsala University. Her expert criticism of various aspects of my book as well as her never-failing interest in my Irish studies have placed me under an obligation which I am happy to acknowledge.

My most cordial thanks are due to Professor Stephen P. Ryan, New Orleans, not only for valuable information about Edward Martyn's manuscript plays but also for his kindness in sending me photostats of some little known Martyn material. I also wish to express my gratitude to Dr. T. P. O'Neill, Dublin, for much useful advice; and to Dr. Thomas McGreevy, Dublin, for friendly encouragement and help.

My sincere thanks go to the staffs of Upsala University Library, the National Library, Dublin, and Olso University Library, who have given full co-operation.

Let me record here, finally, my indebtedness to my wife who in so many ways—and not least in bearing with an overdose of 'Ibsen' in our daily conversation—helped and encouraged me to finish this book.

J. S.

Introduction

One of the most fascinating characters in George Moore's famous auto-biography, '*Hail and Farewell!*', is "dear Edward". Thus the author calls his friend and controversialist Edward Martyn who is the subject, on some immortal pages, of a rather malicious, yet magnificent full-length portrait.

"In 1894," Moore writes in his vivid overture to *Ave*, "Edward Martyn and I were living in the Temple, I in a garret in King's Bench Walk, he in a garret in Pump Court. ... I used to go to Pump Court, sure of finding him seated in his high, canonical chair, sheltered by a screen, reading his book, his glass of grog beside him, his long clay pipe in his hand; and we used to talk literature and drama until two or three in the morning."[1]

Later on, when Edward Martyn was occupying two rooms in Lincoln Place, Dublin, George Moore was in the habit of serenading his friend in the evening from the pavement. The following memorable scene is taken from *Salve* and gives an almost physical impression of the inveterate bachelor in his chaotic study:

"I began to look out for the light above the tobacconist's shop. The light was there! My heart was as faint as a lover's, and the serenade which I used to beguile him down from his books rose to my lips. He will only answer to this one, or to a motive from *The Ring*. And it is necessary to whistle very loudly, for the trams make a great deal of noise, and Edward sometimes dozes on the sofa.

On the other side is a public-house, and the serenading of Edward draws comments from the topers as they go away wiping their mouths. One has to choose a quiet moment between the trams; and when the serenade has been whistled twice, the light of Edward's candle appears, coming very slowly down the stairs, and there he is in the doorway, if anything larger than life, in the voluminous grey trousers, and over his shoulders a buff jacket

---

[1] *Ave* (London 1947), p. 1.

which he wears in the evening. Two short flights of stairs, and we are in his room. It never changes—the same litter from day to day, from year to year, the same old and broken mahogany furniture, the same musty wall-paper, dusty manuscripts lying about in heaps, and many dusty books. If one likes a man one likes his habits, and never do I go into Edward's room without admiring the old prints that he tacks on the wall, or looking through the books on the great round table, or admiring the little sofa between the round table and the Japanese screen, which Edward bought for a few shillings down on the quays—a torn, dusty, ragged screen, but serviceable enough; it keeps out the draught; and Edward is especially susceptible to draughts, the very slightest will give him a cold. Between the folds of the screen we find a small harmonium of about three octaves, and on it a score of Palestrina. As well might one try to play the Mass upon the flute, and one can only think that it serves to give the keynote to a choir-boy. On the table is a candlestick made out of white tin, designed probably by Edward himself, for it holds four candles. He prefers candles for reading, but he snuffs them when I enter and lights the gas, offers me a cigar, refills his churchwarden, and closes his book."[1]

There is, in *Ave*, another famous passage in which Moore satirizes "dear Edward's" avowed muddle-headedness: "He is like Ireland, the country he came from; sometimes a muddling fog, sometimes a delicious mist with a ray of light striking through; and that is why he is the most delightful of travelling companions. One comes very soon to the end of a mind that thinks clearly, but one never comes to the end of Edward."[2]

In a final outburst, towards the end of *Vale*, Moore sums up what might well be called one of the strangest friendships in the history of literature: "There is no doubt that I owe a great deal of my happiness to Edward; all my life long he has been exquisite entertainment."[3] In a typical allusion to the iniquity of Nature,

---

[1] *Salve* (London 1947), pp. 128–129. Cf. the following passage: "Edward is all right if he gets his Mass in the morning and his pipe in the evening. A great bulk of peasantry with a delicious strain of Palestrina running through it." (*Ibid.*, p. 95.)

[2] *Ave*, p. 134.

[3] *Vale* (London 1947), p. 191.

Moore goes on to say: "And I fell to thinking that Nature was very cruel to have led me, like Moses, within sight of the Promised Land. A story would be necessary to bring Edward into literature, and it would be impossible to devise an action of which he should be a part. The sex of a woman is odious to him, and a man with two thousand a year does not rob nor steal, and he is so uninterested in his fellow-men that he has never an ill word to say about anybody. John Eglinton is a little thing; Æ is a soul that few will understand; but Edward is universal—more universal than Yeats, than myself, than any of us, but for lack of a story I shall not be able to give him the immortality which he seeks in sacraments. ... As I understand him he is a temperament without a rudder; all he has to rely upon is his memory, which isn't a very good one, and so he tumbles from one mistake into another. My God! it is a terrible thing to happen to one, to understand a man better than he understands himself, and to be powerless to help him."[1]

From the above quotations which, incidentally, will help us to understand certain aspects of Martyn's drama, it is obvious that George Moore looked upon his friend as his own Sancho Panza. Edward Martyn, on the other hand, lost no time in retorting that Moore had "constituted himself my Boswell". The forbearing playwright was, however, sufficiently provoked to score off George Moore in his satirical play *The Dream Physician* where the tactless biographer, in the obvious disguise of George Augustus Moon, becomes the laughing-stock of everybody.

Now, in spite of the many unforgettable glimpses of Edward Martyn as he appears in '*Hail and Farewell!*', any reader of the memoirs can see with half an eye that the portrait remains a torso in so far as there is practically no account of Martyn's remarkable achievement in the history of Ireland's Literary Renaissance. Besides, whatever information there is, it is almost invariably supplied with a view to making the playwright appear in a comic light.

Edward Martyn's dates are 1859–1923. His father, John Martyn of Tulira Castle, was one of the leading landlords of County Galway. He appears to have been a descendant of the Crusader, Oliver Martin, who landed in Ireland with Strongbow. John Martyn

---

[1] *Vale*, pp. 191–192.

married the daughter of a well-to-do business man who belonged to the peasant class. Two sons, Edward and John, were born in this marriage. Both boys were quite small when they lost their father. Edward Martyn's brother died young and he himself "was to grow up profoundly conscious of his own isolated position as the last survivor of the Martyn family in the county which had once been full of them".[1] Mrs. Martyn had but one ambition. She wanted her son to make a fine career ending up with a suitable marriage. So she sent him to Oxford. She also allowed him to see as much of Europe as he pleased, hoping that one day he would occupy his father's position as one of the principal landlords of the county. Above all she kept planning for his marriage. She refused to accept what other people felt instinctively, that her son was not a marrying man. Yeats, who knew him well, says that "he shrank from women like a medieval monk," adding that "with him died a family founded in the twelfth century. An unhappy, childless, unfinished, laborious man, typical of an Ireland that is passing away."[2] True, no doubt, but hardly the whole truth.

By way of introduction and as a striking contrast not only to Yeats' lament for his dead friend, but also to George Moore's brilliant, though highly prejudiced, portrait of Edward Martyn, one is almost bound to quote the opening lines of Professor Denis Gwynn's remarkable study of the man and the period. "No other Irishman," he writes, "in the various movements which together may be generally described as the 'Irish Revival'—between the eighteen-nineties and the establishment of the Irish Free State in 1921—occupies the same prominent place as Edward Martyn as a connecting link between so many intellectual activities. He was in the peculiar position of being the only Irishman with large private means who was in full sympathy with almost every phase of the Irish Revival. ... But he was much more than the source of money which was indispensable for each new enterprise. He had already made a reputation among men of letters when Mr. W. B. Yeats was beginning to be known as a poet; and it was he who introduced Mr. Yeats to both Mr. George Moore and to Lady Gregory, and obtained their collaboration with him in founding the Irish Literary

[1] Denis Gwynn, *Edward Martyn and the Irish Revival* (London 1930), p. 43.
[2] W. B. Yeats, *The Bounty of Sweden* (Dublin 1925), p. 52.

Theatre which afterwards developed into the Abbey Theatre. It was Edward Martyn who not only provided the money with which the first group of actors were got together, but who also wrote the first play which attracted favourable attention when it was acted in Dublin, and so made the subsequent development possible."[1]

It is part of the tragedy of Martyn's life that this development proved contrary to his own artistic credo as expressed in the famous manifesto that Yeats, supported by Martyn and Moore, issued in 1899 in the first number of *Beltaine*, the official organ of the Irish Literary Theatre. "Norway," it is solemnly announced, "has a great and successful school of contemporary drama, which grew out of a national literary movement very similar to that now going on in Ireland. Everywhere critics and writers, who wish for something better than the ordinary play of commerce, turn to Norway for an example and an inspiration."[2] The pioneering work of the Théâtre Libre and the Independent Theatre is hailed with satisfaction as well as such inexpensive theatres "which associations of men of letters hire from time to time that they may see upon the stage the plays of Henrik Ibsen, Maurice Maeterlink, Gerard Hauptmann, Jose Echegeray, or some less famous dramatist who has written, in the only way literature can be written, to express a dream which has taken possession of his mind."[3]

Now, even if the manifesto seemed to strike a rather cosmopolitan note, it would soon be evident that the apparent identity of purpose of the three collaborators was merely illusory. The main difference might be described as a clash between national and cosmopolitan ideals. Yeats, as well as Lady Gregory, took a real interest in Irish folk-lore, both finding inspiration in the life of the peasantry. They soon became absorbed by the mutual task of presenting to the Irish Theatre the kind of folk drama, coupled with plays of legend and history, which they considered should form the repertory to the exclusion of practically all other forms of drama.[4] "Our movement,"

---

[1] Gwynn, *op. cit.*, p. 13.   [2] *Beltaine*, May 1899, p. 6.

[3] *Ibid.*, p. 6. Yeats' spelling of the names has been left unchanged.

[4] Yeats, it is true, was later to go back on his own principles. Thus, in 1919, he was forced to admit that the scope of the Abbey had been too narrow. By forming the Dublin Drama League with a view to producing famous continental plays, Yeats did tardy justice to the original project of his partners in 1899.

18

Yeats wrote in 1902, in an article in the review *Samhain*, "is a return to the people, and the drama of Society would but magnify a condition of life which the countryman and the artisan could but copy to their hurt. The play that is to give them a quite natural pleasure should either tell them of their own life, or of that life of poetry where every man can see his own image, because then alone does human nature escape from arbitrary conditions."[1]

Such a programme could hardly conform to that of Martyn and Moore who were both well versed in contemporary drama and only too eager to stimulate the production in Ireland of the kind of cosmopolitan drama of ideas which they had come to know and admire during their stay in London. No other member of the Irish dramatic movement had such a first-hand knowledge of the growth on the Continent of the 'independent' theatre as Edward Martyn. According to Malone, he "had known the Théâtre Libre in Paris, the Freie Bühne in Berlin, and the Independent Theatre in London, following their work with the closest attention, as in these experimental theatres he saw the only hope for the literary drama."[2] In 1906 Martyn joined forces with Padraic Colum and other friends in launching a new project. It was called the Theatre of Ireland. The programme of the first night included Seumas O'Cuisin's play *The Racing Lug*, Douglas Hyde's *The Twisting of the Rope* and the fourth act of *Brand*. During the Ibsen Week of 1908 *A Doll's House*, *Hedda Gabler* and *The Master Builder* were performed at the Gaiety Theatre in Dublin by an English Company. "Practically no audience present, however in the front row of the pit stalls I noticed the faithful Ibsenite Edward Martyn—an eager & an appreciative spectator."[3]

Having founded a theatre of his own in 1914, Martyn was in a position to produce his own dramas as well as many new plays by some of his countrymen. But the repertory of the Irish Theatre, as the new venture was called, also included translations of continental masterpieces by Ibsen, Strindberg, Chekhov, Maeterlinck, and

[1] *Samhain*, quoted Denis Gwynn, *op. cit.*, p. 137.
[2] Andrew E. Malone, *The Irish Drama* (London 1929), p. 66.
[3] Joseph Holloway's *A Dublin Playgoer's Impressions*, May 1908. (MS. 1812, p. 503. National Library of Ireland.) I am indebted to Dr. Birgit Bramsbäck for information on this point.

Galsworthy. Chekhov, by the way, was a great favourite with the
Irish dramatist. Both writers looked upon the Northern master as
the great pioneer for the theatre of poetic realism, the kind of inner
drama that they themselves wanted to create. "The whole meaning
and drama of man," Chekhov writes of *Uncle Vanya*, "is in inter-
nal and not in external phenomena."[1] Words that might equally
well stand as a motto for what is best in Martyn's own dramatic
writings.[2]

Although the Irish playwright was in sympathy with Yeats'
new departure, a sympathy that bordered on self-effacement, he
could not fail to notice that from now on the initiative had passed
into the hands of Yeats. It is significant that the rapid disappearance
from the stage of both Martyn and Moore was followed by the
almost simultaneous rise of a new star, J. M. Synge, who soon
brought the Irish drama to the peak of perfection.

Thus it happened that Martyn, for all his enthusiasm and generosity in advancing the ideals of "Irish Ireland", came to play a
rather subordinate, though by no means unimportant part in the
development of the Abbey Theatre.[3] In an unpublished essay, we
find Martyn summing up his situation in words which give us the
clue to his own failure as a playwright: "The dramatist," he writes,
"who practises an art so fascinating to himself (i.e. literary and
psychological drama) is at more disadvantage at present in Ireland
than any other of his brethren. That is why, although I have written

---

[1] B. H. Clark and G. Freedley, *A History of Modern Drama* (New York &
London 1947), p. 413.

[2] It seems likely that certain aspects of Martyn's drama were inspired by the
great Russian. Thus the dream-like atmosphere of *The Heather Field* and of
Maeve recalls a sentence in the opening pages of *The Sea-Gull*. "One must depict
life," Konstantin, the young author, declares, "not as it is, and not as it ought
to be, but as we see it in our dreams." Definitely Chekhovian is the nostalgic
mood of *Maeve* whose delicate heroine keeps yearning for the beautiful things
that are passing. *Grangecolman* no doubt owes something to the author of *Uncle
Vanya* and *The Cherry Orchard*. The hopeless atmosphere of the old manor and
the failure of its lonely inhabitants to break their isolation by really listening to
each other, all this is highly reminiscent of the Russian master.

[3] Martyn was later to refer to "the foundation of the Irish Literary Theatre
in 1899, which was the source of the whole modern Irish Dramatic Movement",
as "the most significant action of my life". (Martyn papers, quoted Denis Gwynn,
op. cit., p. 164.)

more plays than anyone else, which are of course quite useless for commercial purposes, I so seldom get a chance of being produced. If I could have written capable peasant plays, which I could not because they do not interest me, in that the peasant's primitive mind is too crude for any sort of interesting complexity in treatment, I have no doubt I should have found my place naturally in the Abbey Theatre.[1] But I could not, and as the Abbey Theatre could not produce work like mine, which was obviously not suited to their powers (they acted during one week-end *The Heather Field* on the whole so unsatisfactorily that they never attempted it again), I naturally became an isolated figure, who had to depend on my own efforts with amateur players of varied efficiency for seeing my dramas on the stage. ... I produced some plays of Ibsen and of my own with varying results."[2]

On the other hand, Martyn was fortunate in having many friends who were willing, sometimes only too willing, to help him in his literary work. Suffice it to mention George Moore, W. B. Yeats and Arthur Symons to whom Martyn dedicated his first volume of plays. Moore, by the way, wrote an enthusiastic introduction to the book. At a much later date Yeats was to reveal that Moore "had constructed *The Heather Field*, he said, telling Martyn what was to go into every speech but writing nothing, had partly constructed *Maeve*."[3] Sometimes Moore's influence had the effect of a steamroller, as in his re-writing of his friend's political satire *The Tale of a Town*. Yeats supplied Martyn with material for the legendary queen in *Maeve*.[4] At the same time both Yeats and Moore could be frightfully condescending to "dear Edward" as if they envied him the great success he had scored at the beginning of his career. Arthur Symons, the well-known symbolist, lent his exquisite pen to the final phrasing of many passages in *Maeve*, including the beautiful vision.[5] In this connection John MacDonagh should also

---

[1] Apparently Martyn had no very clear picture of the true nature of Yeats' drama, to say nothing of the possibilities of the "peasant play", to use his own contemptuous phrase, in the competent hands of Lady Gregory and, in due time, J. M. Synge.

[2] Martyn papers, quoted Denis Gwynn, *op. cit.*, pp. 158–159.

[3] W. B. Yeats, *Dramatis Personae 1896–1902* (London 1936), p. 44.

[4] Gwynn, *op. cit.*, p. 121.

[5] *Ibid.*, p. 122.

be mentioned. Being both an actor and a dramatist, he played an important part as producer and director of Martyn's Irish Theatre.

The fact, however, that Martyn's original dream of founding a permanent Irish Literary Theatre had not materialized,[1] did not prevent him from carrying out similar theatrical experiments at a later date, ending up, as mentioned above, with the foundation of the Irish Theatre.

"What is my project then?" Martyn asks in the essay already referred to. "It is not original. It is simply to apply the methods of the Abbey Theatre to an organisation of the most talented amateurs for the encouragement by production of native Irish drama other than the peasant species and thereby see if by study and perseverance we may similarly create a bond of young dramatists who will devote themselves to this department of dramatic writing. I feel that however depressed and ruined we may have been by English government and our own inept acquiescence by often playing into the hands of the enemy, we have still some inhabitants left in Ireland besides peasants, and that a theatre which only treats of peasant life can never be considered, no matter how good it may be, more than a folk theatre. Consequently only partially representative of Ireland, it cannot be compared with those other national theatres in Europe which represent so thoroughly the minds of the various countries where they exist. ... Our plays, both native and translations of foreign masterpieces, shall be those not usually acted by professionals. We will also act plays, co-operating with the Gaelic League Players, in the Irish language, from which of course peasant subjects must not be excluded. Here they are fitting in every way. Above all, we will take the greatest pains, so that our performances may be intelligent and finished."[2]

The present investigation will take as its starting-point two of the principal aims of Martyn's new venture, namely the production of non-peasant plays by Irishmen as well as English translations of European masterpieces for the stage. Confining ourselves to Mar-

---

[1] "Edward is sorry," Lady Gregory writes in her diary of September 25, 1921, "he didn't build a theatre twenty years ago, and 'put the key in his pocket.'" (*Lady Gregory's Journals 1916–1930*, edited by Lennox Robinson (Dublin 1946), p. 159.)

[2] Martyn papers, quoted Denis Gwynn, *op. cit.*, pp. 161–162.

tyn's own achievement in the field of drama, we have already seen that he took a special interest in social and intellectual drama as opposed to folk drama.

In the early days of the Irish Revival both Martyn, Moore and Yeats were all united in a mutual effort to do for Ireland what Ibsen and Bjørnson had done for Norway. It is, however, worth noticing that of the three original partners only Martyn remained true, throughout his life, to the gallant slogan of 1899, already quoted above: "Everywhere critics and writers, who wish for something better than the ordinary play of commerce, turn to Norway for an example and an inspiration." Unlike Synge, who concealed his own indebtedness to Ibsen by making negative pronouncements on the Norwegian dramatist, Edward Martyn offers the unique picture of a playwright who does not hesitate to go to the other extreme. With the obvious exception of G. B. Shaw,[1] and, perhaps, James Joyce, it is hard to think of any other Irish author who paid the dues of discipleship more loyally than Edward Martyn.

The very frequency with which the name of the Norwegian forerunner recurs in Martyn's essays, as well as in other pronouncements by him, tells its own tale. No other writer occupies the same place as Ibsen in the papers and articles of the Irish playwright. Apart from some panegyrical declarations, which from time to time would escape him,[2] Martyn left not a few penetrating essays on the Norwegian dramatist and his writings.[3] Visual impressions of some early performances of Ibsen's plays[4] and a life-long study of his drama formed the natural background to Martyn's own literary activities. Having observed that preacher and poet kept struggling for the pen of his beloved master, the Irish playwright instinctively sided with the poet, paying less attention to Ibsen the social refor-

---

[1] Cf. especially *The Quintessence of Ibsenism* (London 1913).

[2] E.g. "Certainly Ibsen is the most original as well as the greatest of dramatists." (Martyn papers, quoted Denis Gwynn, *op. cit.*, p. 144.)

[3] Selections from these essays appear in the present introduction *et passim*. Martyn also wrote stimulating reviews of Ibsen's plays. See for instance "The Recent Performance of Ibsen's *Rosmersholm*" in *The Irish Review*, February 1914.

[4] For a full account of English translations of Ibsen and the spread of his work in England, see Miriam A. Franc, *Ibsen in England*, Boston 1919, Appendices A–B.

mer, who was at that time eagerly discussed by the English public "when the stirring of the bones began in the late eighties".[1]

In one of his essays Martyn draws attention to the fine union of poetry and realism that characterizes Ibsen's prose dramas. "For the way with these wonderful plays," he writes, "where subtle mental poetry finds expression in the most direct realism of speech, as here (i.e. *Little Eyolf*) and in *Rosmersholm* and above all in *The Master Builder*, is to give the sensation of rare harmonies, to produce with their triumphant construction the effect of a symphony where idea grows naturally from idea, where dramatic effects are but the natural outcome of logical combinations of circumstances, where profound knowledge of the human heart and character is set down with such certainty of intellect as may be seen in the lines of a drawing by some great master."[2]

Martyn's analysis of Ibsen's works is no doubt advanced for its time and confirms the impression that the Irish dramatist was not only deeply interested in Ibsen; he had also a first-hand knowledge of his plays and a remarkable flair for the true significance and greatness of the Ibsenian drama.

---

[1] Una Ellis-Fermor, *The Irish Dramatic Movement* (London 1954), p. 5.
[2] Martyn papers, quoted Denis Gwynn, *op. cit.*, p. 142.

CHAPTER I

The Heather Field

Edward Martyn made his *début* as a dramatist in 1899, the very
year in which Henrik Ibsen laid down his pen for ever. *The Heather
Field* formed part of the opening programme of the Irish Literary
Theatre and was first performed at the Antient Concert Rooms,
Dublin, May 9, 1899. It was a greater success with the audience
than Yeats' *The Countess Cathleen* which had been acted the night
before.

The action of *The Heather Field* takes place about the year 1890
in Carden Tyrrell's house on the west coast of Ireland.

Plot

Act I

The scene represents Carden Tyrrell's library. At the back
through open glass folding-doors a small garden is visible, below
which the Atlantic Ocean, flanked by a mountain on the left,
stretches out to the horizon.

Carden's younger brother, Miles, is seated at a writing-table.
He is unable to concentrate upon his studies because of the estrangement that separates Carden and his wife, who have been married
for ten years. Miles confides his trouble to their mutual friend,
Barry Ussher, a wealthy landowner living in the neighbourhood.
It turns out that Ussher had done his best to persuade Carden not
to marry Grace, a beautiful but calculating young woman who only

cared for his money and his position. The power of her influence soon turned Carden, hitherto a charming and engaging man, into a mere shadow of his former self. The first sign of revolt, however, was when Carden took up his work in the heather field to whose reclamation he is prepared to sacrifice everything. Before long he has sunk a fortune in the barren mountain which he has set his mind to conquer. When he makes his first appearance in the play he is about to raise more money to meet the dangerous situation that has arisen as a result of the drainage of the heather field having practically swamped the lands below it. Ussher and Miles fail to persuade Carden to be more careful about the way he spends his fortune. But it is too late. The heather field has already become an obsession with Carden. Life seems to him nothing but a dream from which there is no awakening except in the great mountain field he is trying to bring to fruitfulness. Up in the mountain, followed only by his little son Kit, Carden is able to find himself again as he was in the old days before his fatal marriage. The presence of the boy quickens the magic of the heather field, for Kit happens to be very like his uncle Miles as he looked ten years before.

Faced with his wife, Carden is bound to meet with opposition. But resistance can only make him more determined to carry out his plans. Finally, his own wife declares that she believes him to be mad. The act closes on a bewildered Carden asking himself if there can possibly be a doubt as to which is the reality and which is the dream.

Act II

Grace Tyrrell has asked her neighbours, Lord and Lady Shrule, to lunch. Her husband, however, prefers to stay away in the heather field, busying himself with his great project. Lady Shrule, who really cares for Mrs. Tyrrell, is anxious to help her friend whose rash marriage has always puzzled her. Mrs. Tyrrell objects that Carden was a good match at the time. Besides she had always counted on ruling the roost because of Carden's infatuation about her. But as soon as Mrs. Tyrrell tried to centre Carden's interest too exclusively upon herself, she suddenly became as nothing to him—what he loved was something mysterious, beyond her. According to Mrs. Tyrrell's friend, Carden never loved his wife. Lady Shrule goes so far as to intimate that the Tyrrells were always a queer lot. Carden's father was very eccentric and his mother went quite out of her mind before she died. This is news to Mrs. Tyrrell. It all comes in very handy, bringing grist to her mill. For she is now planning to prevent Carden from ruining his family. It appears that she is actually expecting two doctors who, upon the plea of holding a consultation about the little boy Kit, are going to form an opinion as to the mental state of her husband. Upon his return home, Carden, not taking alarm, informs the doctors of his plans for the reclaiming of waste land. It turns out to be a gigantic project leading up to the forming of a company for buying and reclaiming or reafforesting every inch of waste land in Ireland. The face of a whole country will soon be changed thanks to Carden's creative work. For the stubborn landowner, who cannot endure the dull drudgery of ordinary cultivation of the soil, had gone to great efforts in order to "idealize" farming, until, finally, there came to him the master-thought of the heather field. What really arouses the suspicion of the doctors is, however, Carden's dream philosophy, the voices on the mountain which call him back to his real life, i.e. the life he was leading before he wandered into the present dream. Carden then bids farewell to the company. His friend, Barry Ussher, is left with the delicate task of pleading his cause before the doctors. They eventually yield to his opinion and leave the house without giving Mrs. Tyrrell their final verdict as to her husband's reputed insanity. With suppressed anger Mrs. Tyrrell makes Carden's friend responsible for her failure. Mr. Ussher is, however, prepared to take the consequences. He asks Mrs. Tyrrell if she has considered her own responsibility. To "imprison" a man like Carden would practically mean his death. Mrs. Tyrrell replies that she must protect herself and her child. Hoping that his friend will never know about Mrs. Tyrrell's intrigues against him, Ussher implores her to be patient and gentle with Carden. For she might yet win him back. "It was too late," Mrs. Tyrrell retorts, "from the moment his thoughts first turned to the heather field."

Act III

Having been forced to evict his tenants because of their demands for far-reaching abatements on rents, Carden Tyrrell has become a prisoner on his own estate. He prefers to stay at home since he is no longer able to visit his domains without a police escort for fear of being shot at. Even his little son Kit, the elf of the heather field, fails to make his father stir from his hearth. The boy has just received a nice little pony from the kind-hearted Ussher and rides off to the heather field in order to find some wild flowers for his father. Follows a conversation between Carden and Ussher about the serious state of affairs. Ussher suggests to his friend, who has not taken part in the drainage of the valley for a long time, that they should both set out for a journey and leave everything behind them for a while. But Carden is not in a mood to surrender. As for the work, he stubbornly objects that he can direct it just as well from his room—like Moltke fighting battles from his study! Carden's most difficult task is not, however, to cope with his tenants, but to come to terms with pressing mortgagees. It turns out that he has just sent his brother Miles to the chief creditor asking him not to foreclose until Carden is able to let the heather field. Ussher does all in his power to persuade his friend to come to an agreement with his tenants. But Carden does not feel like complying with their demands, thereby reducing the value of his property. If the worst should come, he declares, I have always the great resource—the heather field! Ussher warns his friend not to pin his faith too exclusively upon a single resource. Besides, Carden is too much of a sportsman to be able to survive for long the dreadful state of affairs that has turned his own home into a prison. Somewhat later Miles brings bad news to his brother. The chief mortgagee has refused to wait any longer. Carden is, of course, paralysed by the blow. But it opens his eyes, if only for a moment. Then, suddenly, he clings to his old vision. "This vulture cannot touch the heather field! My hope—it is my only hope now, and it will save me in the end. Ha, ha! these wise ones! They did not think the barren mountain of those days worth naming in their deed. But now that mountain is a great green field worth more than they can seize, (*with a strange intensity*) and it is mine—all mine!"

Stirred to the bottom of his soul, Carden leaves the room only to run into his little son, bringing with him, not the wild flowers he had been looking for, but a handful of heather buds! And so, with the flowering of the Heather Field, Carden's soul is plunged for ever into the dark waters of madness. The struggle is over. Carden has at last found his lost youth. Everything that has been done in the past becomes undone. Carden's wife becomes Miss Desmond and Kit his brother Miles. The curtain closes on a man who stands as if transfigured, reasserting his idealism, for he has regained for ever the happy hunting grounds of his boyhood when his mind was serene and the world beautiful beyond words: "Oh, the rainbow! Come quick, see the lovely rainbow! Oh, mystic highway of man's speechless longings! My heart goes forth upon the rainbow to that horizon of joy! The voices—I hear them now triumphant in a silver glory of song!"

Theme

The central theme of *The Heather Field* is the fatal clash of dream and reality, of fact and fantasy. The hero of the play clings to his wild schemes with a tenacity that spells disaster. His ideal becomes an obsession, an *idée fixe*, and finally a mania. The conflict is presented in a manner which is clearly reminiscent of Ibsen's treatment of a similar subject in some of his most important plays, notably *The Wild Duck*.

Character

The main conflict of *The Heather Field* is revealed in the development of the protagonist of the drama, Carden Tyrrell. From the point of view of Ibsenian influence on Martyn a close study of the hero of his first play is most rewarding. Ever since he first conceived

the character of Brand, the Norwegian dramatist continued to produce variations of this particular psychological type, i.e. the un-
compromising fanatic and moralist, so that in the end he left a
whole gallery of dogmatists, idealists, dreamers, and visionaries.
Moreover, the insistence upon the individual's loyalty to his calling
is something of a *leitmotif* in Ibsen's works from the early days of
The Pretenders and *Brand* down to his dramatic epilogue *When We
Dead Awaken*. Dwelling for a moment on Brand, comparing him
with Carden Tyrrell, we are bound to notice that there is a certain
similarity in the very dilemma with which both are faced—the
reconciliation of what they consider to be their mission to the
demands of the family. Thus Brand is willing to sacrifice everything, his wife, his child, his social and financial position in obedience to his vocation. Martyn's hero, for all the difference in other
respects, turns out to be equally absorbed by his inner vision.
Opposition can only provoke his innate fanaticism. In pursuit of
his ideal, Carden, like Brand, is ready to sacrifice both his family
and his fortune. True, Carden does not love his wife any longer,
but on the other hand he is deeply attached to his brother and
above all to his little son Kit whom he adores.

This is not to argue that Carden Tyrrell is an Irish Brand. But
Martyn's hero is clearly a descendant not only of Brand but of a
whole group of Ibsenian fanatics, possessed with an *idée fixe*, often
a desperate desire to carry out "the impossible". Like Ibsen's heroes,
Carden is a dreamer of strange dreams, a man haunted by a vision
that in the end turns out to be an illusion. Carden, like so many of
Ibsen's heroes, is pursuing a dimly perceived ideal which can never
be reconciled to stubborn fact and the demands of real life. Like
Brand, like Rosmer, like Solness and Rubek, Carden is bound to sink
under the burden. *L'amour de l'impossible* proves fatal to them all.

Among the works of Ibsen there is, however, one particular
drama which must not be overlooked in this connection. And that
is *The Wild Duck*. In this play, perhaps more than in any other,
Ibsen is engaged on a penetrating analysis of the conflict between
fact and fantasy, dream and reality. Some years earlier he had
solemnly declared that truth and freedom were the *Pillars of Society*.
In *An Enemy of the People*, which precedes *The Wild Duck*, Ibsen
reinforced his statement. The plays that follow, however, represent

a new departure in the literary career of the Northern dramatist. As we shall see, one of the most interesting innovations of *The Wild Duck* is the subtle technique of the play. Before discussing this point, let us for a moment dwell upon the message of *The Wild Duck*. It is contrary to the lesson of the earlier plays. In a letter of June 1884 there is a significant hint at Ibsen's new attitude and the spirit that pervades *The Wild Duck:*

> "I gave up universal standards long ago, because I ceased believing in the justice of applying them. I believe that there is nothing else and nothing better for us all to do than in spirit and in truth to realise ourselves."[1]

And so *The Wild Duck* expresses Ibsen's new standpoint that the happiness of the average man is dependent on his being allowed to preserve his illusions. Already in *Brand* and *Peer Gynt*, it is true, Ibsen had dealt with certain aspects of the same problem. In these earlier plays, however, the great playwright was inclined to consider the conflict from a moral point of view, whereas in *The Wild Duck* the stress is mainly on the psychological aspects of the case. The study of Ibsen's hero, Hjalmar Ekdal, the photographer, exposes a typical day-dreamer who has carried the noble art of self-deception to such heights of perfection that a sudden disenchantment must necessarily spell disaster. The dream-world of Hjalmar Ekdal is primarily founded on his willed belief in himself as a clever inventor, who will soon be the talk of the town. "Ekdal's misfortune," says Dr. Relling, the commentator of the play, "is that in his own circle he has always been looked upon as a shining light."[2] When, through the gratuitous meddling of his old schoolfriend, Gregers Werle, the self-styled inventor is suddenly robbed of his belief in his own superiority, life becomes intolerable and tragedy is close at hand. To quote Dr. Relling once more: "Rob the average man of his life-illusion,[3] and you rob him of his happiness at the same stroke."[4]

---

[1] Letter to Theodor Caspari, dated Rome, 27th June, 1884. *The Correspondence of Henrik Ibsen*. The translation edited by Mary Morison. (London 1905) p. 383.

[2] *The Wild Duck*, Act V, pp. 367–368. All references to Ibsen's plays are to *The Collected Works of Henrik Ibsen*. Entirely revised and edited by William Archer. Vols. I–XII. Heinemann, London 1906–1912.

[3] Lit. "the life-lie".   [4] *The Wild Duck*, Act V, p. 372.

If the reader of this brief analysis of *The Wild Duck* now turns to *The Heather Field*, it will be apparent, from the summary of the plot given above, that there is a definite similarity between the two plays, as regards both subject-matter and character drawing. In the first place both Hjalmar Ekdal and Carden Tyrrell have an innate tendency of talking themselves into believing in the future success of their own fanciful projects. They readily indulge in day-dreams that will never materialize. Mrs. Tyrrell's sneer at her husband: "You imagine yourself the busiest man in the world; and as a matter of fact you have nothing to do"[1] reads like a perfect characterization of Ibsen's self-styled inventor who lies on his sofa all day, inventing nothing except pretexts for doing nothing. When the despotism of reality becomes intolerable, both men take refuge in their respective castles in Spain. Ibsen's hero has a passion for idealizing life in order to make it more endurable. Hence all his talk about being a great inventor whose time is too precious for ordinary work. Turning to *The Heather Field*, the parallel with *The Wild Duck* once more becomes obvious. Hjalmar Ekdal and Carden Tyrrell are birds of a feather. The Norwegian day-dreamer would sooner or later have succumbed to the despotic rules of everyday existence if it had not been for the stimulating principle of "the life-lie". For Hjalmar Ekdal was long buoyed up by his illusions of being a clever inventor. In a similar way his Irish descendant was always out of sorts until finally, after much pondering, there came to him "the master-thought of the heather-field".[2] Like Hjalmar Ekdal he cherished this idea until it became an obsession that finally developed into a mania. In a great speech that recalls Hjalmar Ekdal's grandiloquent ejaculations, Carden Tyrrell admits that he, too, was forced to "idealize" the monotonous existence for which he was clearly not fitted. Hence his extravagant speculation in the heather field, which restores his self-respect and gives him a certain amount of courage with which to face his dreary home life.

TYRRELL. Oh, the work is a glorious one. There is something creative about it—this changing the face of a whole country! None of the humdrum, barn-door work of ordinary farming, with its sordid accompani-

---

[1] *The Heather Field*, Act I, p. 25.
[2] *Ibid.*, Act II, p. 48.

ment of the cattle fair. When from the ideal world of my books those people forced me to such a business, I was bound to find the extreme of its idealisation.[1]

Furthermore, it is worth noting that Martyn sides with Ibsen in stressing the belief that to a man like Carden Tyrrell the perception of reality must necessarily result in mental, not to say physical collapse.

These are the main points of resemblance between Martyn's hero and some of Ibsen's most prominent *dramatis personae*. Further references to Carden's character will be found in the remaining sections of the present chapter.

As for the other persons that figure in Martyn's play, they hardly give the impression of being the children of an abundant imagination. Like some of Ibsen's inferior literary creations the majority of Martyn's people seem to have been invented merely for the sake of argument, to express an idea. Consequently most of these characters are so abstract and stereotyped as to admit of no individual interpretation.

Episodes

In a comparative study of Martyn's works and those of Ibsen it may not be devoid of interest to find out whether or not Martyn's studies in Ibsen have left any traces on his own dramatic output in the form of actual borrowing of parallel or closely related scenes.

In the first place there is the lengthy scene in the second act of *The Heather Field* in which Carden's wife in an extremely painful way tries to persuade the doctors of her husband's insanity. Although this scene appears to have been primarily modelled on a similar episode in Strindberg's *The Father* (1887),[2] it seems to me

---

[1] *The Heather Field*, Act II, p. 48.
[2] A French translation of this play was published in Paris as early as 1888.

that there is also an echo of *The Master Builder*. The more so, as this drama, a favourite with Martyn, left its distinctive mark on the delicate ending of *The Heather Field*. As indicated above, Solness, the Master Builder, and Carden are kindred spirits. What interests us here, however, is the fact that Carden's wife, like Mrs. Solness, believes her husband to be mad. Secondly, both wives provoke their partners until these are forced to admit, if only by a slip of the tongue, that they are actually mad.[1] Furthermore, both men are secretly spied upon by the women. Finally, both wives try to save themselves by seeking the assistance of a doctor.

Another parallel, even more telling than the one just dealt with, is to be found at the very end of *The Heather Field*. For what could be more reminiscent of Ibsen's *Ghosts* than the beautiful scene in which Carden Tyrrell passes over the border-land? Osvald's pathetic cry for the sun[2] the very moment his own intellect is darkened for ever finds an almost exact echo in Carden's triumphant vision of "the rain across a saffron sun"[3] which accompanies the gradual dissolution of his mind.

Finally, there is an undeniable similarity between Carden's great project and that of John Gabriel Borkman. As will appear from the following quotations, Martyn's hero, like Ibsen's financier, dreams of becoming a benefactor to his country by exploiting the riches of Nature.

CARDEN. Wait till you see the profits I shall make. With these I shall extend my works; and with the further profits I shall embark on such a scale of business as in time will enable me to start a company for buying up and reclaiming or reafforesting every inch of waste land in Ireland. ... With the far-reaching usefulness of my projects I must become a real benefactor to the country —[4].

BORKMAN. I wanted to have at my command all the sources of power in this country. All the wealth that lay hidden in the soil, and the rocks, and the forests, and the sea—I wanted to gather it all into my hands, to make myself master of it all, and so to promote the well-being of many, many thousands.[5]

---

[1] *The Master Builder*, Act II, pp. 264–265. *The Heather Field*, Act I, p. 27.
[2] *Ghosts*, Act III, pp. 294–295.   [3] *The Heather Field*, Act III, p. 82.
[4] *The Heather Field*, Act II, pp. 47–48.
[5] *John Gabriel Borkman*, Act II, pp. 247–248.

Thus Carden dreams of doing for Ireland what Borkman had once dreamed of doing for Norway. Like Borkman, Martyn's hero has set his mind on carrying out a gigantic project. Like Ibsen's financier, Carden is fully convinced that the forces of Nature are bound to be controlled by his superior brain.

Technique

Ibsen's dramatic form has long been recognized as one of his most original contributions to the development of modern drama. It was studied with advantage by contemporary playwrights all over the world, even by those who disliked the message of the Norwegian master.

As might be expected from such a keen admirer of Ibsen as Edward Martyn, a careful study of his plays from a technical point of view seems to reveal not a few interesting parallels which strike the reader as being peculiarly suggestive of some of Ibsen's dramatic devices. That this is so becomes apparent already in the work with which the Irish playwright was introduced to the play-going public.

To begin with, the very setting of *The Heather Field* is typically Ibsenian, what with detailed stage-directions for the creation of a double perspective such as open folding-doors leading out into a garden flanked by sea and mountain—an arrangement which corresponds almost exactly to the background of quite a few of Ibsen's plays, notably *The Lady from the Sea* and *Little Eyolf*. As we shall see, the surrounding landscape is furthermore brought to bear on the development of character in a way that recalls some of Ibsen's greatest achievements. Speaking about stage-directions, it is also worth noticing that Martyn adopted Ibsen's novelizing method of introducing his characters to the reading public. Thus Martyn is always particularly anxious to give minute directions as to the exact age and appearance of his *dramatis personae*. In his effort at individualization Martyn at times becomes almost as exacting as the great Norwegian in his claims on scenic representation. For the part of Carden Tyrrell, for instance, Martyn prescribes "a rather powerfully built man of one and thirty, with light hair, spare growth of beard, unsteady eyes, very large forehead, and lower part of face small".[1]

By the irony of fate Martyn's people are often characterized in a far better way by similar stage-directions than by their actual way of talking. For when it comes to individualization by means of dialogue, an art wherein Ibsen excelled, Martyn reveals what is, perhaps, his greatest weakness as a dramatist. It would be practically impossible to point to a single play by Martyn, including *The Heather Field*, which is not marred by an uneven style and stilted dialogue.

Returning for a moment to the background of *The Heather Field*, there is no denying the fact that Martyn, as a great lover of Nature, was primarily inspired by the beautiful scenery that surrounded his own castle in the west of Ireland.[2] But one need not study his first play for long to notice that he went to great efforts and, in my opinion, also succeeded in adopting Ibsen's unerring method of scenic representation of the landscape by the use of dialogue, what French critics with a happy term call *décor parlé*. Thus the heather field, though actually never seen by the audience, pervades the action in much the same way as, say, the fatal mill-race and the sea in Ibsen's *Rosmersholm* and *The Lady from the Sea*.

The Norwegian dramatist was particularly fascinated by the problem of the "displaced person", i.e. the open-air man who by the force of circumstances is compelled to give up his ordinary out-of-door life to pine away in a state of mental uneasiness. Having become prisoner on his own estate, Carden Tyrrell is rapidly reduced to a mere shadow of his former self. His pathetic longing for the sun, the firmament and the sea as well as the open-air life in the mountain and the heather field puts us in mind of Allmers in *Little Eyolf*, returning from the serene life of the hills to his

---

[1] *The Heather Field*, Act I, p. 9.

[2] One of Martyn's visitors, a young baronet from Kent, speaks of "the delightful soft Irish atmosphere, the stroll over the park, down to watch, through circles of cawing rooks, the sun setting over Galway Bay, and those wild rides in the heather-covered mountains ..." (Gwynn, *op. cit.*, p. 60.)

depressing home, and, towards the end of the drama, of Osvald in *Ghosts*, to say nothing of Ellida Wangel and Rebekka West who are both consumed by their innate horizon-fever. Finally, one might draw attention to the obvious similarity between Carden and Borkman in *John Gabriel Borkman*, another of Ibsen's castle-builders, who sits brooding in self-imposed captivity, biding his time.

Furthermore, the forces of Nature are brought to bear on the development of character by means of symbolic suggestion in a manner that is strongly reminiscent of Ibsen's effective use of symbolism. Most telling in this respect is perhaps the expressive allegory of Nature revenging herself upon the intruder—the very key-note of the play. As will be seen from the following quotations, this allegory serves a double purpose, being applied both to the hero of the drama and to the heather field itself. By way of parallelism Martyn draws attention to the danger of trying to meddle with the forces of Nature which cannot be subdued with impunity.

USSHER. There are some dispositions too eerie, too ethereal, too untamable for good, steady, domestic cultivation, and if so domesticated they avenge themselves in after time. Ah, foolishly his wife and her friends thought they were going to change Carden to their model of a young man, but the latent, untamable nature was not to be subdued. Its first sign of revolt against suppression was when he began this vast work in the heather field.

...

If heather lands are brought into cultivation for domestic use, they must be watched, they must have generous and loving treatment, else their old wild nature may avenge itself.[1]

This effective way of character revelation apparently owes something to the new, highly developed technique which characterizes the symbolic plays of Ibsen's later period. It is significant that in *The Wild Duck*, where all the main characters are interpreted in the terms of the wild bird that figures in the play, there is also a similar reference to the revenging power of Nature as the one quoted above. Hjalmar Ekdal's father, the old bear-hunter, assails Gregers Werle with questions as to the present state of his old hunting grounds.

---

[1] *The Heather Field*, Act I, pp. 8–9.

EKDAL. Are the woods fine up there now?
GREGERS. Not so fine as in your time. They have been thinned a good deal.
EKDAL. Thinned? (*More softly, and as if afraid.*) It's dangerous work that. Bad things come of it. The woods revenge themselves.[1]

To make the parallel even more striking, old Ekdal's parrot-like repetition of "the woods avenge themselves",[2] when, at the end of the drama, he learns about little Hedvig's tragic death, is echoed almost exactly in the words that Martyn puts on the lips of Carden's friend the moment the dreadful truth begins to dawn upon him: "The vengeance of the heather field."[3]

Before leaving the question of Martyn's Ibsenian way of character revelation by means of symbolism, a few words must also be said about the voices that haunt Carden throughout the play. These "voices from the past" form a link between Carden and his youth, the influence of which he cannot escape. The realistic explanation of this supernatural phenomenon is the same as the one given by Ibsen in *The Master Builder*, namely that both Solness and Carden are overstrung. As previously with Ibsen, these voices symbolize the irrational, the inexpressible, all that in the long run is more important to man than anything that can actually happen to him. Just as there is a meaning in the harps that fill the air at the death of the Master Builder, there is a meaning in the "triumphant voices" which Carden hears "in a silver glory of song!" In both cases the celestial music accompanies and interprets the final liberation of a soul in agony.

Thus both Ibsen and Martyn have attained, by similar means, "that silvery beauty which survives in the human heart, which we see shimmering to the horizon, leading our longings beyond the world, and we hear it in our hearts like silver harp strings, sounding seemingly of themselves, for no hand is by".[4]

There are many other technical similarities between *The Heather Field* and some of Ibsen's plays, as for instance the subtle use of dramatic irony which is so characteristic of Ibsen's scenic method.

---

[1] *The Wild Duck*, Act. II, p. 256.
[2] *Ibid.*, Act V, pp. 395-396.
[3] *The Heather Field*, Act III, p. 79.
[4] George Moore, preface to *The Heather Field*, p. xxvi.

Mrs. Alving in *Ghosts* tries to save her son's life by idealizing the memory of his dissipated father. Thus Osvald is brought up on a white lie which in reality embitters his whole life, for he cannot rid himself of the completely erroneous idea of having contracted the fatal disease from which he is suffering. Hjalmar Ekdal's marriage is ruined by the gratuitous meddling of his best friend; Hedda Gabler's desperate suicide draws the following comment from the middle-aged cynic of the play: "Good God!—people don't do such things"[1]—and so on.

In *The Heather Field* the final catastrophe is brought about by a similar revelation of the truth. The scene which describes Carden's fatal meeting with his little son, offering him a handful of heather buds, and Carden's staring at them as if he had seen so many ghosts, derives much of its effect from the very irony of the situation which is quite in keeping with Ibsen's achievement by similar means.

Most important of all technical similarities between Ibsen and Martyn is the general structure and the poetic atmosphere of the works of both playwrights. In a penetrating essay on the character of Ibsen's drama the Irish author makes the following statement:

> "He has invented a whole new world for drama, even more interesting than any of the old. He has invented the drama of the mind, where outer action is all subordinate to the tremendous strife of wills and emotions, which work out to their inevitable conclusions with a mastery of art that intellectually delights a thinking audience. ... It would be well for many more to study this great national and, because so great, a world dramatist, whereby they might be led to understand his un-approached excellences, and be put out of conceit with their delusions about their own. They need not agree with Ibsen's opinions, some of which I am far from accepting myself. His opinions do not affect the quality of his technique, which is so original and beyond all rivalry, and rewards the severest study."[2]

And so Martyn in writing *The Heather Field* paid homage to the great Norwegian pioneer, adopting, in his first play, some of Ibsen's fundamental creative principles of the drama. Like his master, Martyn succeeded "where hitherto no modern English dramatist has even dreamed that drama was to be found".[3]

---

[1] *Hedda Gabler*, Act IV, p. 185.
[2] Martyn papers, quoted Denis Gwynn, *op. cit.*, pp. 144–146.
[3] George Moore, preface to *The Heather Field*, p. XXVII.

Some of Martyn's comments on the achievement of Ibsen might well be applied to *The Heather Field*. For is it not a noteworthy attempt, also, at paving the way for the intellectual drama, "the drama of the mind", as Martyn puts it, "where outer action is all subordinate to the tremendous strife of wills and emotions, which work out to their inevitable conclusions".

Indeed, the outer action of *The Heather Field* is reduced to a minimum. Whatever there is of drama, is to be found in the tremendous struggle of the hero for self-realization. Finally, Martyn's play is characterized by that particular blend of apparent realism with genuine poetry which is immediately recognized as typically Ibsenian.

On the other hand, the Irishman's first play must not be dismissed as being merely the work of a dramatist in leading strings. To complete the picture, it is only fair to add that the author of *The Heather Field* offers his readers a highly interesting commentary on purely native conditions. Thus we get a vivid impression of the difficulties that faced Irish landlords towards the end of the last century. The rise of the Land League under Parnell, who wanted to restore the land to the peasants, soon forced landowners all over the country to engage in a back-to-the-wall struggle for their existence. According to Denis Gwynn, "evictions and strikes against payment of rent became more and more frequent, as the Land League spread through the west; and before long, Edward and his mother were to have the bitter experience of having their land-agent shot at near Tulira".[1]

Thus it turns out that Martyn was able to draw on personal experience when he set about writing his first drama. The hero of *The Heather Field* no doubt expresses the extreme landlord views that the author is known to have held at the time of the agrarian unrest. But it is worth observing that Martyn opposes his own hero in the figure of Barry Ussher who tries to persuade Carden Tyrrell to adopt his own policy of voluntary settlement with the tenantry. Tyrrell refuses and is no longer able to visit his domains for fear of being shot at by his own tenants. Thus, although the land question is merely touched upon in Martyn's drama, the personal accent is unmistakable.

---

[1] Gwynn, *op. cit.*, p. 54.

40

The same holds true of the Irishman's critical attitude to women and married life. Here there is a fundamental difference between Ibsen and Martyn. With Maeve as the one notable exception, it is hard to think of a single important female character in the works of Edward Martyn with whom the author is really sympathetic, or, it must be admitted, with whom the reader may sympathize. Sometimes, as in *The Heather Field*, the antagonism between man and wife becomes so accentuated as to remind one of Strindberg. In this respect it seems to me that Martyn's negative attitude to women links him with the Swedish playwright rather than with Ibsen who simply excels in his portraits of great women.

Even at the time of its first production, *The Heather Field* was admired for its firm construction as well as for its subtle use of symbolism which neutralized the realism of the work and gave it the third dimension of poetry. Martyn's drama was regarded as an original attempt at doing for Ireland what Ibsen had already done for Norway. To quote Moore once more, *The Heather Field*

"was the first play written in English inspired by the examples of Ibsen. ... A play that possesses qualities of balance, design, sequence is a work of art and will hold its own in any company; and although 'The Heather Field' will seem small by the side of 'The Wild Duck,' it will hold its own by the side of 'The Wild Duck,' or 'Macbeth,' or 'Hamlet,' just as a housewife by Peter de Hoogh will hold its own by the side of the 'Marriage Feast' by Veronese, or the 'Entombment of Christ' by Titian, or the 'Last Judgment' by Michael Angelo".[1]

---

[1] George Moore, preface to *The Heather Field*, pp. XXII–XXIII.

CHAPTER II

Maeve

When Martyn published his first drama, *The Heather Field*, in the year of 1899, this play was accompanied by *Maeve* with an introduction to both plays by George Moore. *Maeve* was first performed at the Gaiety Theatre on February 20th, 1900.[1] According to Boyd, *The Heather Field* and *Maeve* "were the two plays which constituted the greatest successes of the Irish Literary Theatre".[2] Bourgeois, on the other hand, states that "little enthusiasm was raised" by the production of *Maeve*.[3]

Plot

The scene of *Maeve* is laid in the west of Ireland. "The action," Martyn says, "takes place during the present time about and at O'Heynes Castle among the Burren Mountains of County Clare in Ireland."

At his castle, situated in a romantic landscape, old Colman O'Heynes is dragging out a tedious existence supported only by his two daughters Maeve and Finola. Planning to rise in the world once more, the impoverished old man has gone to great efforts to

---

[1] Lady Gregory, *Our Irish Theatre* (London & New York 1913), p. 261.

[2] E. A. Boyd, *The Contemporary Drama of Ireland* (Dublin & London 1918), p. 13.

[3] M. Bourgeois, *John Millington Synge and the Irish Theatre* (London 1913), p. 121.

42

secure the marriage between Maeve and a wealthy Englishman, Hugh Fitz Walter, whom she does not love but whose riches will enable the old Prince to re-establish himself as "The O'Heynes" among the gentry of County Clare. It turns out, however, that the young Princess has already lost her heart to a mysterious lover who visits her in her dreams together with the legendary heroes and heroines of Ireland's remote past.

Torn between her visions of "the beautiful dead people" and a sense of filial duty to her poverty-stricken father, Maeve is comforted by her old nurse Peg Inerny. This strange old woman feeds the imagination of the young girl with tales of "the other people". Thus Maeve has come to believe that Peg herself changes from the tattered old peasant woman, shunned by the neighbourhood, into the great Queen Maeve. In her plight the lonely Princess looks upon Peg as a medium who may enable her to communicate with the strange lover that haunts her dreams. And so the old hag finds the visionary girl only too responsive to her seductive charm. That same night which happens to be her wedding-eve Maeve accompanies Peg to the mountains to meet the great figures of Ireland's legendary past and the noble lover of her vision. The glory of the frosty moon-lit night on the mountain side holds her spell-bound for several hours. Midnight has just passed when Maeve, deeply stirred by the overpowering beauty of her vision, finds her way back to the old castle, bathed in moonlight.

Instead of going to bed she resorts to a window of the castle from where she can see the mountain range that encircles the ruined abbey, Goban's round tower and the legendary old cairn of Queen Maeve. Without heeding the piercing cold of the night, the young Princess settles herself comfortably at the open window and soon becomes lost in reverie.

In her trance the visionary girl sees the strange procession of Queen Maeve and her attendants rising out of the mysterious cairn. As they approach the castle, the call of the other world becomes irresistible. On its way back the number of the procession is increased, for the spirit of Maeve passes with the Fairy Queen and her retinue into the realm of Tír na n-Óg, the country of the ever-young.

Early in the morning Finola goes to prepare her sister for her

43

wedding with the young Englishman, only to find the bride sitting
cold and lifeless at the open window. At last Maeve has met her
noble lover and found "rest in beauty".

Theme

The main themes of the two plays which constituted Martyn's
dramatic *début* strike the reader as being closely related to each
other. In each case we are confronted with a visionary idealist
unable to cope with the cold, materialistic world of reality. Carden
Tyrrell's dilemma, like that of Maeve, is emphasized by the striking
contrast between the free open-air life on the heights and the dull,
depressive life in the valley. In other words, the conflict recalls one
of the themes that appear with clock-like regularity in the works of
Ibsen, from his early poem *On the Heights* down to *When We Dead
Awaken*.

One of Ibsen's principal themes is his insistence upon the individual's loyalty to his calling. Both *The Heather Field* and *Maeve*
offer interesting variations of this theme set against an Irish background. Like his Norwegian forerunner, who developed the psychological play to perfection, Martyn stresses the inner drama, presenting in *Maeve* a soul in agony. Trying to live up to the ideal of
her visions, Maeve is torn between two incompatible worlds. As
with Ibsen in similar conflicts, it is the choice that matters in man's
struggle for self-realization. Like Ibsen, Martyn knew exactly
how to draw the portrait of a self-absorbed dreamer and idealist so
as not to alienate the sympathy of the discerning reader. Thus
George Moore, in an admirable comment upon *Maeve*, arrives at
the following interesting conclusion: "Although shorn of all common humanity, our sympathy is with her as it is with Carden
Tyrrell, and we cry, 'Believe in your warrior of long ago, and let
go by you the young Englishman who seeks to rob you of your
dream;' and to triumph thus over common instincts and infect the

reader with sympathies and longing which lie beyond the world is surely to succeed where hitherto no modern English dramatist has even dreamed that drama was to be found."[1]

Character

The analysis of *The Heather Field* revealed among other things that character drawing was hardly Martyn's strong point. His failure might have been less apparent had he been able to keep his characters at arm's length. As it is, Martyn's work suffers from the author's stereotyped grouping of the figures in different sets, i.e. the idealists with whom he sympathizes and the materialists who merely provoke his indignation. This tendency is so strong that even his best plays, like *The Heather Field* and the one under discussion, are marred by the author's fatal habit of reading his strange prepossessions into his characters.

Turning to the portrait of Maeve, which in my opinion represents Martyn at his very best, this complicated figure does not at first strike the reader as being particularly Ibsenian. To begin with, it must be admitted that Maeve does not seem to be modelled on any definite character in the works of the Norwegian playwright. This is hardly surprising for a man of Martyn's extensive reading. Being well versed in the drama of Ibsen, the Irishman was in a position to pick and choose significant features from more than one of the old master's plays.

Ibsen was duly praised for his penetrating studies of half-grown, precocious girls, sometimes dreaming and sensitive like Hedvig in *The Wild Duck*, sometimes high-strung and fanatical like Hilde Wangel in *The Master Builder*. In spite of Martyn's different aim, elements of both these types were incorporated into his picture of Maeve. Like Ibsen's young heroines, the Irish girl creates her own dream-world, jealously protecting it against intrusion from abroad. Furthermore, Maeve's imagination, like that of Hedvig, is secretly

---

[1] George Moore, preface to *The Heather Field & Maeve*, p. XXVII.

nourished by her eager study of the book treasures in the mysterious garret.[1] Finally, both girls, sensitive and vulnerable though they be, turn out to be strong enough to stand up for their ideals, facing death rather than linger in a world of selfishness and materialism.

The spiritual superiority of Maeve together with her heroic struggle for self-realization are apt to surprise in a character conceived by a notorious misogynist. This somewhat unexpected exception to the rule is, of course, mainly due to the patriotic background and purpose of the play. But I feel convinced that it also owes at least something to the author's studies in Ibsen. For it is a well-known characteristic of the work of the great Norwegian that practically all the women of his plays stand head and shoulder above the weak, irresolute men whose lives they dominate.

Like so many of Ibsen's heroes and heroines, Maeve is carried away by an inner urge that cannot be suppressed without danger. Her feelings prove stronger than the voice of the intellect.

"I must! I must; thus a voice commands me deep in my soul,—and I will obey that voice."

These words form the opening lines of Ibsen's first play, *Catilina* (1850). Throughout the dramatist's later work the voice of the rebel Catilina is echoed by a surprisingly great number of his leading characters, particularly the women, who usually act from a similar impulse of being compelled to revolt in one way or another.

Martyn's heroine is torn between two worlds. She cannot live without her love, she cannot die without her soul. In the end filial duty is overcome by the young girl's longing for self-realization. Yielding to her beautiful vision of Ireland's legendary past, Maeve renounces her family and the world to find peace in the cold arms of her unknown lover.

What Martyn shows us is a soul in agony. Like Ibsen's rebellious Nora she is aware of her duty to her family. But, again like Nora, it dawns upon her that she has an even greater duty to herself. Naturally I do not want to imply that Maeve is an Irish Nora. My sole object is to draw attention to a remarkable similarity as regards the spiritual conflict of *Maeve* and that of not only *A Doll's House*

---

[1] Cf. Mary Bruin in Yeats' *The Land of Heart's Desire*.

but of a great number of Ibsen's plays where the main theme in the Norwegian's own words is "the struggle which all serious-minded human beings have to wage with themselves in order to bring their lives into harmony with their convictions".[1]

As often with Ibsen's characters, Martyn's heroine is gradually isolated by her extravagant dream, irreconcilable as it is with actual conditions and the demands of ordinary people. Indeed, Maeve has much in common with those men of Ireland's dim and distant past "who believed so much in the soul, and so little in anything else, that they were never entirely certain that the earth was solid under the foot-sole".[2]

But, and this is another characteristic trait, Maeve is not merely an idealist. She is also an aesthete unable to come to terms with life for she is above the sordid engagements of the world. To save her individuality the visionary girl disregards the demands of life and resorts to a kind of spiritual escapism. Shut up in the ivory tower of her dreams, Maeve deliberately turns her back upon those around her lest human considerations should spoil her beautiful vision of the other-world. By adopting an essentially aesthetic attitude towards life Maeve succeeds in regaining her spiritual freedom and integrity. Hence her strange way of looking at life as if in a mirror that has little more than a pale reflexion of the world to offer her lonely soul. As a matter of fact it would seem that Maeve is primarily a product of the literary aestheticism of the 1890's.

The following two quotations illustrate the conflict of the heroine better than many words. To begin with, we have Maeve's disillusioned remark on the effect of her visions:

MAEVE (*wistfully*). Such beautiful dead people! ... I see them now, and I see others who lived long before them, and are buried in that green cairn. Oh, I am dying because I am exiled from such beauty.[3]

Towards the end of the drama Martyn focuses attention upon the dilemma of Maeve by putting the following credo on her lips: "Form is my beauty and my love!"[4]

---

[1] Letter to Bjørn Kristensen, dated Munich, 13th February, 1887. *The Correspondence of Henrik Ibsen* (London 1905), p. 412.

[2] *Samhain* 4, 1904, quoted W. B. Yeats, *Plays and Controversies* (London 1923), p. 123.

[3] *Maeve*, Act I, pp. 88–89.   [4] *Maeve*, Act II, p. 122.

These words strike the very key-note of the play which simply abounds with "beauty from the past", "greatest beauty", "immortal beauty of form", and "rest in beauty". Thus we are once more reminded of the fact that in spite of the genuine Irishness of the drama, Maeve herself is by origin in many respects a product of the literary aestheticism of the time.

But it would be a definite mistake, I think, to read her words merely like an effective motto. For is it not possible, without being fanciful, to look upon this outburst of *l'art pour l'art* as a private confession of the author? With Maeve Martyn shared an overweening passion for the beauty of form. But unlike his heroine, who managed to live up to her vision, Martyn was only partly successful when it came to presenting his own dreams in a literary form.

The conflict between the aesthetic and the ethical recurs from time to time in the works of the Norwegian playwright. With him it is something of a *leitmotif*, spanning a period of almost exactly half a century. One of the "trolls" Ibsen kept fighting throughout his life was the aesthete. Over and over again, the dramatist exposes the man who remains a spectator looking at life "through the hollow hand" in order to improve the perspective rather than descend from the heights of self-imposed isolation. Thus the perils of indulging too freely in aestheticism are repeatedly emphasized by Ibsen in a long series of works, from the important poem *On the Heights*, written as early as 1859–60, down to the fin-de-siècle cult of aestheticism in, say, *Hedda Gabler* with the heroine's insistence upon "death in beauty", and *When We Dead Awaken* with its *Einsame Menschen* to quote the title of one of Hauptmann's most Ibsenian plays. *When We Dead Awaken* was the Norwegian's "dramatic epilogue". Only here, with death close upon his heels, did Ibsen realize that he himself had never lived. "The hollow hand" had beaten him. And yet he tells his readers that if he were allowed to live his life over again, he would once more choose art rather than life. For in the words of Martyn's heroine, "form was indeed his beauty and his love!"

In spite of much apparent dissimilarity of subject and intention, the fact remains that Martyn's heroine is also finally caught by "the hollow hand" and frozen to death for a mere fancy in a way which recalls Ibsen's treatment of similar conflicts.

48

Summing up, one might say that the literary origin of a character like Maeve can be traced back to different sources. Primarily she is no doubt a daughter of her native country, inspired by Martyn's own knowledge of Irish folklore.[1] Besides, there is more than an echo of Yeats' early play *The Land of Heart's Desire* where "stars walk upon a mountain-top" and fairies "dance upon the mountains like a flame".

On the other hand, Maeve is undoubtedly also a product of the 1890's, whereas Martyn's framing of the problem, including his strong emphasis on the aesthetic conflict, as well as his subtle treatment of the heroine's mental development must be looked upon as proof positive of actual influence from the Ibsenian drama of ideas.

So much for the literary reminiscences that went into the portrait of Maeve. As for the minor characters of the play, it cannot be denied that they are even more stereotyped than those of *The Heather Field*. Peg Inerny is the one notable exception. For this strange old woman is one of the very few subordinate parts that Martyn managed to individualize to such a degree that it really sticks in your mind.

As in the case of Queen Maeve and her young namesake, Martyn was able to draw from native sources for his fine characterization of this repulsive, yet strangely fascinating woman who believes that she is a queen "when in faery". According to Yeats, Peg Inerny existed in real life. In the essay already referred to Yeats writes: "Biddy Early, who journeyed with the people of faery when night fell, and who cured multitudes of all kinds of sickness, if the tales that one hears from her patients are not all fancy, is, I think, the origin of his Peg Inerny; but there were, and are, many like her."[2]

It is, however, worthy of observation that Martyn confided to Yeats "that he knew nothing, or next to nothing, about the belief in such women as Peg Inerny among the Irish peasants. Unless the imagination has a means of knowledge peculiar to itself, he must have heard of this belief as a child and remembered it in that unconscious and instinctive memory on which imagination builds".[3]

---

[1] See e.g. W. B. Yeats' important essay "Maive and Certain Irish Beliefs", *Beltaine*, February 1900.

[2] W. B. Yeats, *op. cit.*, p. 14.

[3] *Ibid.*, p. 14.

It seems to me, however, that the portrait of Peg Inerny may have been partly inspired by a similar character in one of Ibsen's later plays.

At the time of Martyn's dramatic *début*, *Little Eyolf* was one of the most recent dramas by the hand of the Norwegian master. Now, there is one thing in particular that singles out this play, published as late as 1894, from the majority of Ibsen's other works, namely the introduction of the curious Rat-Wife. The short appearance of this sinister character in the first act of the play, immediately produces an uncanny atmosphere that lingers throughout the drama.

In *Maeve* the introduction of Peg Inerny has a very similar effect. Even a cursory reading of this part reveals some interesting points of resemblance with that of the Rat-Wife. True, both women are introduced for different symbolic reasons. But the psychological correspondence between the two characters is unmistakeable. The strange behaviour of the old women, always at their busiest in the dead of night, tells its own story. Thus both seem to nodalize the forces of the supernatural and the gruesome. The Rat-Wife and Peg Inerny feed the imagination of little Eyolf and Maeve with their siren song of sleep and dream. Finally, both the boy and the girl succumb to the lure of the old women who bring about their premature death.

Technique

As shown by the previous investigation, Martyn's drama, like that of Ibsen, is deficient in external action. Thus Moore was perfectly right in pointing out that in *Maeve* "human emotion is the whole of the play".[1] As a matter of fact this very aspect of Martyn's fairy play constitutes the nearest approach to the Ibsenian theatre. Like Ibsen, the Irish playwright is not primarily

---

[1] Moore, *l.c.*, p. XXVII.

interested in the outer world. The conflict of the soul is their drama. Characteristically enough, *Maeve* is subtitled "a psychological drama". It is typical of Martyn's way of working that, like Ibsen, he chooses for his theme an emotional conflict, more particularly a soul at a crisis. Furthermore, the main tension of the play is caused by the ultimate choice of the heroine. For Martyn, and here we are once more reminded of his great forerunner, is primarily absorbed by the struggle for self-realization of his leading characters.

Examining *Maeve* from the point of view of dramatic method, one cannot help noticing Martyn's close adherence to some of Ibsen's principal technical rules, such as the importance of selection and concentration. Hence the careful minimization of external action. Hence also the small cast. Numbers would have stifled the tragedy.

As to the power of individualization, an art in which the Norwegian playwright excelled, we have already seen that Martyn was only partly successful. Generally speaking, one might say that the plays in which Martyn appears to advantage, notably *The Heather Field* and *Maeve*, derive much of their strength and dramatic effect from the influence of Ibsen's scenic method. It is, after all, only natural that the technical innovations that the Northern master passed on to contemporary playwrights all over the world should have left their mark on the works of such a devout Ibsenite as Edward Martyn.

Apart from what has already been said above, one is often struck by Martyn's extensive use of symbolism. Once more the strains were caught up from the Norwegian dramatist.

In a previous study[1] the present writer has discussed a peculiar aspect of Ibsen's scenic method, i.e. the author's strange habit, when one of his characters is drawn to another, of making the latter symbolic.[2] Thus Ellida Wangel in *The Lady from the Sea* is attracted by the Stranger and the Sea, and Solness in *The Master Builder* by Hilde and Youth. Of particular interest in this respect are two other characters, namely Brand who is haunted by Gerd

---

[1] *Ibsen and the Beginnings of Anglo-Irish Drama*. I. *John Millington Synge* (Upsala 1951), p. 21.

[2] See Henning Kehler, "Studier i det ibsenske Drama", *Edda*, V (1916), p. 97.

51

and the Ice Church, and little Eyolf, magnetically drawn to the Rat-Wife and Death.

In the same mysterious way Martyn's Maeve is hypnotized by her noble lover, the Ice Prince, and by his realm of Beauty that unfolds in Death. Although this "prince of the hoar dew" never appears in the play, he certainly makes his presence felt in a much stronger way than Maeve's anaemic English suitor. In the extremely moving end of the drama, Maeve's true lover clutches the girl in his ice-cold arms, for he is Death, leaving the scene "completely white with a thick coating of hoar frost".

Ibsen, we have seen, often introduced symbolic characters to give the climax of the action an illusion of inevitability. Sometimes, as in *Rosmersholm*, the symbol does not materialize. But the white horses that haunt the old family estate and the fatal mill-race by which Rosmer and Rebekka are finally engulfed no doubt serve the same purpose of stressing the inevitable character of the double suicide at the end of the drama. Furthermore, this kind of symbolism introduces an element of ambiguity which adds to the fascination of the drama.

Investigating Martyn's play from a similar point of view, it is interesting to find that in writing *Maeve* the author resorted to almost exactly the same technical device. The mysterious "day-ghost" that haunts the heroine with its "wistful pleading" is obviously but a projection of Ibsen's supernatural beings, invented to serve as a link between two worlds as well as to prepare the reader for the tragic end.

In this connection it is worth noticing that in *Maeve*, as also in *The Heather Field*, Martyn adopts his master's habit of providing a rationalistic explanation of the supernatural element that dominates the drama. Peer Gynt, to take an early example, "runs his head against a rock, falls and remains stretched on the ground"[1] before he meets with the Green-Clad Woman, the Trolls and the Boyg. In other words, Peer's accident accounts for his hallucinations, including his strange visit to the King of the Dovre-Trolls.

Similarly the white scarf which is so inseparately associated with Rebekka West acts as a connecting link between the inhabitants of

[1] *Peer Gynt*, Act II, p. 65.

Rosmersholm and the ghosts, i.e. the White Horses that haunt the place. Here the white scarf of the mistress of Rosmersholm affords a possible explanation of the ghostly disturbances as we are given to understand that the old servant may have mistaken the woman in white for the spectral horses.

Turning to Martyn, the great dream-scene in which Queen Maeve summons the young girl to Tír na n-Óg is no doubt a mere projection of the heroine's last dream as death gently steals upon her in the bitter cold of the night.

According to Allardyce Nicoll, "Martyn's real strength is seen to lie in this strange union of reality and of the supernatural. Few dramatists have succeeded as he did in welding together into a complete whole these two spheres".[1] Few dramatists maybe, but here again Ibsen is surely to be counted among the pioneers of this particular kind of drama. The author of *The Wild Duck, Rosmersholm, The Lady from the Sea* and *The Master Builder* was bound to attract a man like Martyn, inducing him to try his own hand at a similar work. For in these plays the union of fact and fantasy is masterly attained. Here the ageing master deals with the fascination of Nature and the supernatural in terms of symbolism in a way that does not spoil the illusion of reality. This is precisely what Martyn set out to do and also managed to achieve at the beginning of his career when he was still chiefly under the spell of the great Norwegian.

With the passing of the years, however, Martyn's drama takes on a new aspect. Although still faithful to Ibsen, the Irish playwright tends to abandon his early highly poetic themes in order to concentrate his efforts on various topics of everyday life. But in so doing, Martyn unfortunately betrays an increasing preoccupation with some of the less attractive features of the Ibsenian drama. In *Maeve*, however, there is as yet no sign of the cold realism, not to say melodrama, that left its mark on Martyn's later works.

Before leaving the subject of symbolism in *Maeve*, a few words must also be said about Martyn's treatment of a well-known Irish theme, i.e. the harp-motif, to be found not only in *Maeve* but also in *The Heather Field* and linking both plays technically to *The*

---

[1] A. Nicoll, *British Drama* (London 1949), p. 418.

Master Builder. Like Solness, both Carden Tyrrell and Maeve hear voices and melodies from another world. Although the harpers are actually introduced in *Maeve*, whereas the music is only heard from above in the two other plays, the dramatic significance of this particular device remains the same. The soft music is simply indispensable in all the plays as a means of symbolizing the inner drama. In *Maeve* the harps are admirably tuned to the serene mood of the heroine the moment her soul—all passion spent—passes over the border-land.

In spite of Ibsen's strong hold on Martyn, the Norwegian master did not reign supreme. We have already seen that *Maeve* was inspired by different sources, both native and foreign. Maurice Maeterlinck, for instance, developed the inner drama to perfection in a series of plays published in the 1890's. The dream-like atmosphere, the static situation and the symbolism of these exquisite works no doubt appealed to the author of *Maeve* who may be said to move within the same sphere as the Belgian dramatist. It needs stressing, however, that the lofty idealism of Edward Martyn's early plays forms a striking contrast to the extreme pessimism of Maeterlinck's *théâtre statique*.

As early as 1892 Yeats published his first drama, *The Countess Cathleen*, to be followed in 1894 by his beautiful fairy play *The Land of Heart's Desire*. The heroines of both plays are brought to a premature death by their love of Ireland and things Irish. Thus Countess Cathleen sells her own soul in order to save the lives of her countrymen, whereas Mary Bruin sacrifices wedded love for her still greater love of fairydom—the land of heart's desire.

No doubt symbolic elements from both these plays went into the writing of *Maeve*. As a matter of fact Yeats' description of Martyn's play as a symbol of "Ireland's choice between English materialism and her own natural idealism, as well as the choice of every individual soul"[1] reads like a synopsis of *The Countess Cathleen*. On the other hand, it is only fair to add that Yeats himself, while writing his one-act play *Cathleen ni Houlihan*, seems to have been inspired by his friend's powerful portrait of Peg Inerny.[2]

---

[1] W. B. Yeats, *Beltaine*, February 1900, p. 3.

[2] Cf. C. Weygandt, *Irish Plays and Playwrights* (London 1913), p. 94.

Martyn's treatment of the landscape is another aspect of *Maeve* that calls for special attention in a study of the author's indebtedness to Ibsen. The scenery of *Maeve* is that of western Ireland and gives the impression of being modelled on the beautiful surroundings of Martyn's own castle, situated in this part of the country. But, and this is one of the most significant technical parallels to the Ibsenian drama, the manner in which the landscape is brought to bear on human emotions is undoubtedly reminiscent of Ibsen's scenic method. The same applies to Martyn's successful way of introducing the landscape by means of dialogue.[1]

With Ibsen Nature, in true romantic style, was frequently treated as a kind of symbolic supplement to the action. This holds true of the majority of his plays, particularly those written in the '80's and the '90's, such as *Ghosts, Rosmersholm, The Lady from the Sea, Little Eyolf,* and *John Gabriel Borkman.* In other words it is characteristic of Ibsen's technique that the settings are constantly brought to harmonize with the subject of the play. Those that treat of freedom and truth and personal integrity very often take place in the open air, preferably on mountain heights or on the seaboard. On the other hand, Ibsen's gloomy interiors, still the object of much carping criticism, were generally reserved for his plays of social reform in which the stuffy atmosphere serves as a striking contrast to the brightness of the exterior.

In *Maeve* there is a similar correspondence between the visionary heroine and the serene beauty of the surrounding landscape. In the first act the wistful young girl sits brooding among the ruins in the saffron sunlight of the evening waiting for the vision of the beautiful dead people to take possession of her responsive mind. Thus the ruined landscape is skilfully brought to bear on the mood of the young Princess, accentuating at the same time the dramatic conflict of the play.

The scene of the second act is laid outside the old castle the night before Maeve's wedding. Again there is a perfect harmony between character and setting. Technically, this act derives much from the last act of *Brand.* Here the art of defining character in terms of symbolical scenery is brought to perfection. The cold,

---

[1] Cf. above, *The Heather Field*, p. 35.

ascetic hero stands out against a background of ice and snow. The play ends on a note of symbolism. In a final effort to live up to his own motto, *All or Nothing*, Brand climbs the great glacier. At the sight of God's clear sky the cold ice in Brand's tormented soul begins to melt. But his new vision comes too late. Brand reaches the heights once more only to meet his death in the cold arms of the Ice Church as he is swept away by an avalanche.

In *Maeve*, the death-scene of the heroine is built up on much the same lines. As with Ibsen the setting is allowed to play its own significant part in the drama. The frosty night, the cold moon wandering among the lonely mountains, the leafless ash trees, the hoar frost, "the Northern lights of Tirnan-ogue", the grey light of dawn, all these details are cleverly worked out to provide a symbolical background for the triumphant passing of the cold, ecstatic, "beautiful ice maiden".

To complete the analysis, a few words may be quoted from one of Martyn's essays dealing with Ibsen and touching on *Maeve*: "I should like to know the modern dramatists who have since made old-fashioned the art of Ibsen? Who are they who have caught its least excellence, to say nothing of improving on it? I thought that I had developed something from it in my *Maeve*, where I made a girl pine and die for a lover who had no existence, and gave it a semblance of truth. Ibsen was so great, so far before his time, that up to this the best dramatist since is but a pigmy compared with him."[1]

---

[1] Martyn papers, quoted Denis Gwynn, *op. cit.*, p. 145.

CHAPTER III

The Tale of a Town

Completed in the summer of 1899 and published with *An En-chanted Sea* in 1902, *The Tale of a Town* was first produced by the National Players in 1905. In a prefatory note to this "comedy of affairs in five acts" the author makes the following statement: "There was an adaptation of THE TALE OF A TOWN called THE BENDING OF THE BOUGH made by Mr. George Moore, with my consent, for the Irish Literary Theatre performances in 1900." 'Adaptation', by the way, is hardly the right word, because in rehashing the play Moore deliberately disregarded his friend's original intentions.

"With the published version of *Maeve* and the production of the *Heather Field* to go upon, who would have predicted *The Tale of a Town?*"[1] In these words a well-known authority on the Irish dramatic movement sums up what seems to be a general attitude among critics towards Martyn's third drama. The same author devotes several pages to a comparison between Martyn's play and Moore's *The Bending of the Bough* in order to show the superiority of the latter work.

Having studied both plays, I find it difficult to accept such a verdict. In the first place Moore, for all his virtuosity as an artist, was primarily a novelist. When he chose to dabble in play-writing he was invariably let down by his Muse. "In credibility of action," Williams writes, "Mr. Moore may have improved upon his original; but just where the author is strongest in his novels he is weakest in *The Bending of the Bough*. It is a colourless production, its dialogue largely in the air and devoid of local characteristics—a play made in the study about people whom the author has not known intimately."[2] Secondly, Moore himself was aware of his own failure as

---

[1] Ellis-Fermor, *op. cit.*, p. 38.
[2] Harold Williams, *Modern English Writers* (London 1918), p. 201.

shown by the following apology: "The Comedy, entitled *The Bending of the Bough*, was written in two months, and two months are really not sufficient time to write a five-act comedy in."[1]

Many years later even Yeats had to admit that "*The Bending of the Bough* was badly constructed, had never become a single thought or passion, but was the first dramatisation of an Irish problem."[2] Why Irish? Yeats seems to have forgotten that Moore laid the scene of *The Bending of the Bough* in Scotland, thereby completely missing the point of *The Tale of a Town* which is a satire upon Irish conditions. Poor Martyn! Not only was his own play suppressed by his own friends. He also suffered the humiliation of seeing his original idea exploited at the hands of a fellow-countryman who was no more at home in the realm of drama than he was in his own native country. In my opinion Ernest A. Boyd, the well-known historian of the Irish Literary Renaissance, hit the nail on the head by saying that *The Bending of the Bough* "is *possibly*[3] a better written play, but is not, therefore, a better Irish play."[4]

Plot

The scene of Martyn's "comedy of affairs" is laid in a small coast town in the west of Ireland. Up to the present the town has prospered because it happens to be the nearest port in Europe to America. When the play opens we learn, however, that a rival English town, Anglebury, by the use of bribes has deprived the Irish of their American line of steamers. The authorities of the Irish town "were to receive a percentage on all harbour rates in Anglebury, where the shipping was known to be enormous". But —and this is where the conflict begins—so far the Irish have not

---

[1] *Samhain*, 1901, quoted Boyd, *op. cit.*, p. 22.

[2] W. B. Yeats, *Dramatis Personae 1896–1902* (London 1936), p. 48.

[3] The italics are the present writer's.

[4] Boyd, *op. cit.*, p. 25.

been blessed with a single penny. Enter the young hero of the play, Alderman Jasper Dean. Denouncing the sordid intrigues of the authorities of the English seaport, as well as the treachery of some of his own colleagues who, it appears, are not above taking bribes from the English, Jasper Dean manages to unite the Corporation in a final attempt to save the town from further decline. But it is too late. The English have all the trumps in their hand, for Jasper Dean is engaged to an ambitious young girl who happens to be the niece of the Mayor of Anglebury. She tells Dean that she has no intention whatever to bury herself in Ireland. If he wants to marry her, he had better forget his country—"this poor mean place"— and go with her to England which she depicts as a land of "riches and prosperity". At first Dean puts up a gallant fight for Ireland: "I love this poor mean place better than your England that has made it poor and mean. But it will not remain so. We are at last united, and we shall enforce payment of those riches we know are our due."

But it soon turns out that Jasper Dean has been sufficiently corrupted by his future wife and by her well-to-do set to give up his leadership and betray his own town.

*

There are many reasons why the student of Ibsen's influence on Martyn should pay special attention to *The Tale of a Town*. It is the Irishman's first attempt at social satire in a middle-class drama. Here as elsewhere Ibsen had been the great emancipator with plays like *Pillars of Society*, *A Doll's House*, *Ghosts*, and *An Enemy of the People*.

Apparently Martyn had a first-hand knowledge of Ibsen's social drama when he set about writing his own Tale of a Town. In any case the finished play, immature though it is, strikes the reader as being cast in practically the same mould as, say, *An Enemy of the People*. Although Martyn's love intrigue has nothing whatever to do with Ibsen's drama, the fact remains that both works develop on much the same lines. The very subject of *The Tale of a Town* links the play with *An Enemy of the People*. As in Ibsen's drama the scene is laid in a small seaside town. The action of both plays centres on a similar problem. The authorities of either town stand the immediate risk of being cut off from their principal source of income, the kind of business that has made their town a regular gold-mine. In *An Enemy of the People* the threat against the municipal Baths, symbol of the town's prosperity and progress, sets the play going in precisely the same way as the loss of the American packet station in *The Tale of a Town*.

The use of the same middle-class material no doubt accounts for some of the parallels between the two plays. Definitely Ibsenian, however, is the way in which Martyn manages to produce a genuine small town atmosphere. The reader is confronted with a world of chattering busybodies and perpetual turncoats. Like his master, the Irish playwright attacks the "lokale forholde", above all social hypocrisy and social climbing.

The upbringing of Martyn's young hero connects him with two of Ibsen's best known characters. To explain the weakness of Jasper Dean, the Irish dramatist informs his readers that the orphan boy has been brought up by a couple of muddleheaded aunts, who have done their best to spoil him. Now, this very constellation seems to have been extremely popular with Ibsen who made effective use of it not only in *The Wild Duck* but also in *Hedda Gabler*. The appearance of the ubiquitous aunts of *The Tale of a Town* produces the same nonsensical atmosphere as the coming and going of Aunt Julia in the home of Tesman and Hedda Gabler. Martyn's hero is also linked up with *An Enemy of the People*. To be sure, Jasper Dean is no Dr. Stockmann. But he is introduced into the play for the same sake of contrast that characterizes *An Enemy of the People*, i.e. the contrast between an idealistic hero, who is the only person that really loves his town, and the "damned compact majority" of miserable timeservers and ruthless placehunters.

Sometimes an Ibsenian note creeps into the dialogue of Martyn's play. Listen to the following discussion between three of the Aldermen and the Town Clerk in the first act of *A Tale of a Town*. It evokes the Puddletonian atmosphere of *An Enemy of the People* with its vivid picture of the pen-and-ink war in the columns of the *People's Messenger* and the hullabaloo about the Doctor and his mission.

FOLEY. In honour and conscience I feel bound to take some action at the meeting to-day.

CASSIDY. Whether you obtain general support or not, Alderman Foley, will largely depend upon the nature of your action.

FOLEY. You have read my article in the "Weekly Denouncer"?

KIRWAN. It was full of fury, as usual, against the enemies of our town.

FOLEY. The sense of our wrongs fills me with uncontrollable indignation. It is nothing but the sense of our wrongs that keeps me before the public at all.

CLORAN. Indeed, Alderman Foley, the people do say that you have a mission among them.[1]

The satire of both plays is directed against those who go with the flock. Says Aslaksen, the printer, to Dr. Stockmann: "It's always well to have the majority with you, Doctor."[2] And Hovstad, the editor, joins in the chorus: "The majority always has right on its side."[3]

Turning to Martyn's play, we find that the author merely substitutes "the winning side" for "the compact majority" of *An Enemy of the People*. Thus Jasper Dean is constantly urged to "take care and keep on the winning side".[4] ... "To be sure, Jasper —the winning side is always in the right."[5]

Then there is the conflict between the people and the authorities. Hovstad, the editor, is a man of humble origin, a fact that has given him "ample opportunities of seeing what the lower classes really require".[6] A self-made man, Hovstad has no high opinion of the leading men of the town. He arrogantly declares that "we can get on without these august personages".[7]

In *The Tale of a Town* Mrs. Costigan, the charwoman, voices the opposition in a similar way.

Mrs. COSTIGAN. Oh, you're a proud man to be town clerk; but I can tell you this Corporation you think so fine, isn't respected much in the town.

---

[1] *The Tale of a Town*, Act I, pp. 11–12.
[2] *An Enemy of the People*, Act II, p. 49.
[3] *Ibid.*, Act IV, p. 134.
[4] *The Tale of a Town*, Act IV, p. 94.
[5] *Ibid.*, p. 84.
[6] *An Enemy of the People*, Act II, p. 47.
[7] *Ibid.*, p. 46.

CLORAN. You are, no doubt, a sound authority as to the feeling of our town, ma'am.

MRS. COSTIGAN. I'm in the way of hearing many complaints, Mr. Cloran; and believe me if you don't begin to do the people some good, none of you will long remain where you are.[1]

It needs stressing that the Irish playwright leans heavily on Ibsen in his handling of the tumultuous scenes which form such a characteristic part of the plays under discussion. It is hardly a coincidence that the climax of both *An Enemy of the People* and *The Tale of a Town* is a stormy 'political' meeting resulting in street demonstrations with an aggressive mob flinging stones through the windows of the home of the hero.

In his play Ibsen made a drunken man interrupt the meeting at short intervals.

A Drunken Man (*at the main entrance.*) I'm a ratepayer, so I've a right to my opinion! And it's my full, firm, incomprehensible opinion that—

Several Voices. Silence up there!

Others. He's drunk! Turn him out! (*The drunken man is turned out.*)[2]

It is interesting to find that Martyn uses exactly the same trick in one of the most effective scenes of his play. The big meeting of the fourth act is held in the principal hotel of the town. And here Mrs. Costigan is introduced and turned out with the same precision as Ibsen's drunken man.

MRS. COSTIGAN (*having meanwhile repeatedly helped herself to the liquor*). Who's talking of dynamiters?
...

CLORAN. For shame, woman—out you go. Come along—

MRS. COSTIGAN. Hooray! I'm the voice of the people. Hooray—what—you Corporation—are you turning out the people? I'm a respectable woman—

(*She is hustled out by Cloran ...*)[3]

*

So much for the common pattern of the two plays. To complete the analysis, mention should also be made of the manner in which

---

[1] *The Tale of a Town*, Act I, p. 6.
[2] *An Enemy of the People*, Act IV, pp. 127-128.
[3] *The Tale of a Town*, Act IV, p. 97.

Martyn differs from the Northern master. *The Tale of a Town* happens to be an excellent illustration of the subject, for it is an early example of the kind of drama Martyn would write when thrown entirely upon his own resources.

To begin with, the reader of *The Tale of a Town* is struck by a certain lack of proportion of the play. It is as if the author of the previous dramas had suddenly forgotten the importance of such vital dramatic principles as elimination and concentration. He gathers a rich material but, unlike Ibsen, he does not know how to sift it. *The Tale of a Town* is laboured and top-heavy simply because the author insists on cramming more into his play than it can actually hold.

Faulty individualization is another weakness of Martyn's drama. The author is at his best with only a small group of characters. The handling of an extensive cast like that of *The Tale of the Town* is definitely beyond his power. In vain does he struggle to get his personages at arm's length. Most of them remain marionettes moved by clockwork.

The Norwegian playwright on the other hand studies his *dramatis personae* until he knows all about them, including their way of dressing and talking, their characteristic traits and habits as well as their way of acting and reacting in a certain situation. This power of individualization endows Ibsen's characters with the kind of inner life that immediately captivates an audience.

Turning to *The Tale of a Town*, this is precisely where the Irish dramatist fails to convince his readers who have to put up not only with an anaemic hero but also with an endless group of minor characters who are merely there to make the wheel go round.

Unlike Ibsen, and unlike most of his Irish fellow-dramatists, Martyn did not often master the art of writing effective dialogue. The trouble with *The Tale of a Town* is that "the talk of the town" does not ring true. Although he knew Ibsen's plays only through the mist of translations, the Irish disciple was always full of admiration for the variety and veracity of the master's dialogue which seemed to him not only poetic in its realism but also beautifully tailored to the character.[1]

---

[1] Cf. Martyn papers, quoted Denis Gwynn, *op. cit.*, p. 148.

But Edward Martyn, for all his enthusiasm about the theatre, was hampered in his own writing by a certain lack of spontaneity which made it difficult for him to strike the right note of everyday conversation. George Moore, it is true, complimented the author of *The Tale of a Town* on "a certain improvement in the dialogue".[1] But he was merely praising with his tongue in his cheek. The whole play, he added, was so bad that it could not attract "any possible audience—Irish, English, or Esquimaux".[2] The plot of *The Tale of a Town* is interesting enough, but the dialogue is as longwinded as it is stilted and crude. For try as he may, Martyn never approached true dramatic speech. "No politicians," Weygandt writes, "even when egged on by their envious womankind, would ever give themselves away as do these of 'A Tale of a Town'. They are as frankly self-revelatory as if they were characters in a morality play."[3] It did not occur to Weygandt that Martyn may well have had some similar idea in his mind. A glance at the cast of *The Tale of a Town* informs us that the author invented symbolical names for a surprisingly great number of his characters. Hardman, the English Lord Mayor, and his plutocratic niece, Miss Millicent Fell, are already mentioned. To these may be added Joseph Tench, the Irish Mayor, as well as Murphy, Foley and Leech, Aldermen of the Corporation.[4] This particular device is repeated in *The Place-Hunters*,[5] a one-act comedy that brings before us such formidable characters as The Right Hon. Steppingstone Feathernest, Fencesitter Fisher and Lord Kilcooly. In my opinion Martyn deliberately uses this very artifice in order to enhance the satirical effect of the plays.

Martyn's satire illustrates another important difference between the two playwrights. It seems to me that the Irishman was born with a grievance against the world. There is a strong connecting link between the comparatively young man who made his literary

---

[1] *Ave*, p. 127.

[2] *Ibid.*, p. 127. Cf. Yeats' criticism, quoted above, of George Moore's *The Bending of the Bough*.

[3] Weygandt, *op. cit.*, p. 89.

[4] Ibsen, by the way, was fond of the same trick. But it stands to reason that the true significance of most of his characterizing names must have escaped the Irish dramatist.

[5] Published in *The Leader*, July 26, 1902.

début in 1890 with the all-destroying prose satire *Morgante the Lesser* and the author of *The Dream Physician*, a drama published almost a quarter of a century later.

Martyn's indignation is genuine enough. But, unlike Ibsen, he does not know how to sugar his pill. Where the Norwegian playwright mixes his scorn with subtle humour, Martyn has little else to offer his readers but scorn and contempt. The satire of *The Tale of a Town* is so clumsy and, above all, so exaggerated as to destroy at once the illusion of reality that characterizes the opening scene of the play. The author's satirical weapon recoils like a boomerang and he himself appears utterly devoid of Ibsen's sympathy and pity for humankind.

And yet, when all is said the fact remains that Martyn's "comedy of affairs" was breaking fresh ground. *The Tale of a Town* marks a new departure not only in the author's own dramatic output but also in the field of Irish drama which had till then been somewhat limited in its scope.

CHAPTER IV

An Enchanted Sea

As mentioned above, Edward Martyn published his second volume of plays in 1902, containing two very different dramas: *A Tale of a Town* and *An Enchanted Sea*. The latter work was first produced by the Players' Club at the Antient Concert Rooms, Dublin, April 18, 1904.

Plot

Act I

At the old family estate of Fonthill, situated on the Irish west coast, Mrs. Rachel Font wields the sceptre in her own ruthless way. From a modest position as a peasant's daughter she has made her way into society by means of a cleverly planned marriage. When the play opens Mrs. Font's dominating position is threatened, however, by the fact that both her husband and her son are dead, so that the estate has come to belong to her young nephew, Guy Font. But Mrs. Font is the boy's guardian and in that capacity she is still in a position to feather her own nest.

Trying to arrange a fashionable marriage between her daughter Agnes and Lord Mask, a young, highly educated friend of the family, Mrs. Font will stick at nothing to get rid of the lawful owner of Fonthill who stands between her and her ambition. Tradition has it that "one of the first Lord Masks married a sea fairie. He brought her to Mask Castle, where she lived in an upper room of a tower. But she never could rest there, because it was not by the sea. So she was always coming down here to Fonthill and haunting the coast." One day, legend goes on to say, "this sea fairie went back to the sea, and was never heard of again".

When the curtain rises she has, however, just been seen at Mask Castle, and it is rumoured among the superstitious inhabitants of the coast that the present owner of the castle will be the last Lord Mask. Like the sea fairie from whom he is believed to be descended, Lord Mask cannot live at his own castle because it is too inland. So he comes down to Fonthill to be near the ocean and to meet his young friend Guy, who has lived so long by the sea that it has become part of his being. Having lost his parents at an early age, this strange boy has been reared among the peasants who have taught him their language and initiated him into their primitive customs and beliefs. Nature has endowed Guy with a strange second sight that stirs up in him such beautiful visions of the ocean that he is looked upon by his noble partner, Lord Mask, as the timeless genius of the sea.

Guy's strong hold on the young lord threatens, however, to upset Mrs. Font's ambitious plans. She starts speaking ill of the boy before Mask and her own daughter. Insinuating that Guy was sent down from school for drowning his school-fellow, Mrs. Font hopes to put Mask on his guard against his young playmate who keeps drawing him to the sea and to the sea fairie whose willing instrument he is. Lord Mask refuses, however, to give credit to such a preposterous accusation and is warned by Mrs. Font that Guy will do to him—"what he has done before".

At the same time Mrs. Font tries to persuade her daughter that Guy is a changeling occupying the place of the real Guy, whom the fairies have taken. According to Mrs. Font, Guy "is one of those evil spirits, the Fomors, who haunt the land and seek human victims for the sea".

To save Lord Mask, Mrs. Font resorts to a dangerous scheme. Murder is in her mind as she mutters the sinister warning that brings the act to an end: "Those who belong to the sea should go back to the sea."

Act II

Guy takes his friend Mask to the mysterious sea-caves at Fonthill, and the young lord is deeply impressed by the splendid world
of Manannan, the Celtic sea-god. Mask is taken in by the boy's
visions because they seem to answer his own Hellenistic dream
which has hitherto failed to materialize. "Your life·of vision," he
tells Guy, "has awakened for me the genius of the Antique! ...
Your genius has made me see in Ireland my dream of old Greece.
... We both found our lesson book in the sea. ... The enchanted
sea of Hellas taught me to find an enchanted sea." His last words
are echoed by Guy speaking in subdued reverie: "This is an enchanted sea."

But their plans for a "Celtic Revival" are soon interrupted by
Guy's guardian. To secure the fortune and to save the young lord
from what she considers to be his evil spirit, Mrs. Font no longer
hesitates to get rid of the lawful owner of Fonthill. Pretending
affection for Guy, she suggests that the boy show her the sea-caves
—alone! In vain does Agnes plead with her mother not to carry
out her plans the true purpose of which she alone suspects. Headed
by Guy, who is only too anxious to please his aunt, Mrs. Font sets
out on her sinister errand—"to give a sea-fairie to the sea-caves".

Act III

The action takes place outside the entrance to the sea-caves.
Mrs. Font's movements have been watched by two peasants planning to murder her because of her reckless treatment of the tenantry. From their hiding-place they could see Mrs. Font enter the
caves with Guy and come back alone. Having found out her dreadful secret, the two peasants remain hidden behind the rocks biding
their time.

Meanwhile, Mrs. Font is confronted with her daughter and
Commander Lyle who is in love with Agnes. To secure an alibi
Mrs. Font pretends that she has sent Guy up to fetch her a shawl
because she felt chilly in the caves. But before long Mrs. Font is
driven out of her positions. To begin with, Lord Mask brings back

the cap that Guy had been wearing when he was last seen with his aunt. "He gave it to me from the sea. ... He seemed as if he wanted to speak, but he faded away into a receding wave. ... I saw the cap floating near me, and as I knelt down to take it, he rose and gave it to me from the sea. ... I can never leave it (the sea) again. It is an enchanted sea! ... He stood between me and the shadows ..."

Although Mrs. Font is quite upset by Lord Mask's evidence, she makes bold enough to suggest once more that he marry her daughter. "If by some ill luck he (Guy) is dead, would you not like to live always in this beautiful demesne by the sea? You might then very easily make it yours." But this time Mrs. Font has aimed too high. Lord Mask suddenly realizes why she has always hated Guy. "Mrs. Font—I understand you at last. Now I know why everyone fears you. I begin to fear you myself for the first time in my life."

Left alone with her daughter, Mrs. Font uses all her will-power to force Agnes to yield to her plans. "I tell you, child, I would willingly bear the pains of hell, if only I could see my daughter married to a lord." Horrified at her mother's wickedness, Agnes refuses to obey her. There follows a long dispute which is finally interrupted by the reappearance of the two peasants. They are now in a position to prove that Guy has been murdered and Mrs. Font is caught in her own trap. "Your life of wickedness is stopped at last. ... We shall be avenged on you, Rachel Font. When we next meet, you will be in the dock, and we will hang you."

Act IV

A prisoner in her own house, Mrs. Font has not given up all hope to unite Agnes and Lord Mask. But all her scheming comes to an abrupt end at the sudden news of Mask's tragic death. Driven mad by the loss of Guy and haunted by his voice, Mask has gone back to the sea. He continues to look for the boy until one day, standing on the rocks where once he had seen his dead friend, the young lord is overwhelmed by a big wave and carried out to sea by the undertow. "The sea fairy was at Mask Castle indeed", is Mrs. Font's only comment as she stands paralysed by this final blow. Beaten at her own game, she retreats to that part of the hall which Guy has turned into a gymnasium. As the police come to arrest her, they find that she has anticipated events by hanging herself from the landing of the great staircase of Fonthill. It turns out that the rope round her neck is the same that Guy used for a swing. So in the end the dead boy has had his revenge.

Taking Agnes under his wing, Commander Lyle pronounces the moral of the play: "This lonely sea was suited to the visionaries who have passed with their visions away. ... You who have awakened to real life, can find no place here."

Theme

The *leitmotif* of *An Enchanted Sea* is, as the title indicates, the fascination of the sea and the hypnotic influence it exerts upon the human mind. Thus the very theme of Martyn's drama invites comparison with Ibsen's *The Lady from the Sea*. Because in this play, too, the attraction of the sea is felt as a secret undercurrent from the very beginning of the drama. In Martyn's own words: "*The Lady from the Sea* gives expression to that yearning and enchantment which the ocean has for certain natures. An enchanted sea! ... The illimitable Atlantic with all its mystery and beauty calls to us. ... And Ibsen likewise is haunted by the same yearning beauty. Far away, exiled in inland Munich, he craves for the sea, and when in 1887 he returns to it, he gives vent to his enthusiasm and all his homesickness in this exquisite play, *The Lady from the Sea*."[1]

---

[1] Martyn papers, quoted Denis Gywnn, *op. cit.*, pp. 146–147. Cf. Martyn's preface to H. B. O'Hanlon's drama *The All-Alone*, published in 1919. "*The All-Alone* is a drama of the sea. Its idea is the vague charm and longing which the sight of the ocean and the phantasmal life on board sailing-ships awaken in the human heart. The fatality which results from an overmastering obsession by this, or any other mental passion, is more deadly than that from animal passion. In it lies material for the most awful tragedy." (Preface p. VII.)

Naturally the theme as such was by no means monopolized by the Northern playwright. "If objection be made to 'The Enchanted Sea' as a reflection of 'The Lady from the Sea,'" Weygandt writes in his book on the Irish drama, "it can be replied that the call of the sea that may not be resisted is as old as the heart of man. Sea fairies, mermaids and mermen, and the voice of the waters tugging as irresistibly on the tired spirit as the undertow on the body tired with long swimming, are in Gaelic literature from the beginning, and before Mr. Martyn had written of the sea enchantment it had lent its charm to many of the stories of 'Fiona Macleod.'"[1] True, but the point is that there seem to be very few Irish *plays* dealing with this particular theme. Drawing attention to Synge's *Riders to the Sea* and the drama under discussion, Bourgeois comes to the following conclusion: "To speak only of the Irish school itself, we know only of two sea-tragedies: *The Racing Lug*, by 'Seamus O'Cuisin,' and *The Storm*, by Hugh Barden."[2] Under these circumstances it is hard to overestimate the importance of *The Lady from the Sea* as a literary source of inspiration to both Martyn and Synge.[3] But here as elsewhere Ibsen's originality is to be found not so much in the selection of a particular subject as in his own highly individual treatment of the theme he chooses to dramatize.

Character

It is hardly to be expected that Martyn's drama of the sea with its melodramatic action and poor psychology should be of any particular interest to the student of the author's indebtedness to

---

[1] Weygandt, *op. cit.*, pp. 85–86.

[2] Bourgeois, *op. cit.*, p. 159, note. He might, perhaps, have added Yeats' *The Shadowy Waters*.

[3] See the present writer's analysis of Synge's plays, particularly *Riders to the Sea*. This drama was published in 1904, the very year that saw the first performance of *An Enchanted Sea*.

Ibsen. The resemblance of subject is undeniable. Is there any similar connection between the two playwrights from the point of view of character drawing?

Examining the cast of Martyn's play, we may at once dismiss the majority of the characters as being either too vague or too stereotyped to merit individual discussion. In fact, the only two persons that need detain us here are Guy, the owner of Fonthill, and Mrs. Rachel Font, his aunt and guardian. The latter is undoubtedly Martyn's most powerful woman character. Here the misogynist tendency, noticeable in the early portrait of Carden Tyrrell's wife in *The Heather Field*, suddenly becomes predominant. As a character Mrs. Rachel Font is obviously conceived very much on the same lines as some of Ibsen's most dominating women like Rebekka, Hedda Gabler and Hilde Wangel. Naturally Martyn's heroine cannot stand comparison with any of these complicated characters. For it cannot be denied that the fine psychological qualities which one associates with a successful literary portrait are as conspicuously absent from the rather monotonous study of Mrs. Font as they are present in the Ibsenian trio mentioned above. But Martyn's heroine is nevertheless intimately related to this group of strong-willed women. They are all driven by an almost hysterical thirst for power and a fatal desire of playing with other people's lives until suddenly things take a new turn and they are caught in the network of their own scheming. Having staked everything on one card—and lost, Mrs. Font, like another Rebekka or Hedda Gabler, rises to the occasion and eludes justice by becoming her own executioner.

If objection be made that these parallels offer no conclusive evidence of foreign influence, it is interesting to observe that many years later Martyn again exploited almost exactly the same Ibsenian pattern. As will appear from the chapter dealing with *Grangecolman*, the author's pitiless study of Catharine Devlin turns out to be even more closely modelled on the Norwegian prototype.

Then there is the young boy Guy Font. He is an ambiguous character, naive and precocious, young and old at the same time— a living link between this world and the manifestations of the other-world. Primarily this strange child, whose spirit is lost in the waves of the sea, no doubt embodies the author's nostalgic vision of a dateless dream-world, built up on the ancient glories of the Gael and the Greek. The fact that the boy also reflects Martyn's own intense love of Irish scenery merely adds to the strange fascination of this lovable character.

But this alone does not explain the complex nature of Martyn's young hero. What makes Guy Font such an intriguing character is above all his mysterious background and the way in which he displays his supernatural powers. Brought up among the peasants of the west coast of Ireland, the boy has got the sea literally in his blood. So much so that Mrs. Font actually believes him to be a "changeling" belonging to the realm of the sea people.[1] Not only does Martyn stress Guy's intimate relationship with the sea. He has also endowed him with a secret power of bringing other people under his spell, opening their eyes to the beauties of his own world of sea enchantment.

This is precisely where the Ibsenian influence comes most clearly to the fore. Bearing in mind Martyn's special fondness for *The Lady from the Sea*, which he once called a "beautiful prose poem drama",[2] it is hardly surprising that he should have been sufficiently impressed by the appearance of the mysterious stranger in that play to realize that he could use him for his own purpose in the shape of Guy Font. Thus Mask is held by Guy's supernatural power in much the same way as Ellida Wangel, "the lady from the sea", is captivated by the hypnotic power of the Stranger. Ibsen's heroine tells her husband, Dr. Wangel, of the seaman's "unfathomable power over my soul".[3] — Similarly Guy's tutor speaks of his "extraordinary powers for a boy only fifteen years old",[4] adding that "he manages to impose his will on people ... Persons of the same temperament as his".[5] And Mrs. Font asks Lord Mask: "Why is he always leading you away to the sea?"[6]

The fascination of the Stranger and the spell of the sea make Ellida restless in her own home, which lies too far from the coast. Her husband is full of sympathy: "You cannot endure your sur-

[1] *An Enchanted Sea*, Act I, pp. 150–151.
[2] Martyn papers, quoted Denis Gwynn, *op. cit.*, p. 144.
[3] *The Lady from the Sea*, Act II, p. 235.
[4] *An Enchanted Sea*, Act I, p. 125.
[5] *Ibid.*, pp. 130–131.
[6] *Ibid.*, p. 140.

roundings here. The mountains oppress you and weigh upon your spirits. There is not light enough for you here—the horizon is not wide enough—the air not strong and stimulating enough for you. ELLIDA. There you are quite right. Night and day, winter and summer, it is upon me—this haunting home-sickness for the sea."[1]

Turning to Martyn's play, we are struck by a similar development of character. For Guy, and all that he symbolizes, makes it equally impossible for Lord Mask to remain at home: "Oh! I cannot live down there at Mask. It is too inland.[2] ... I should always feel lonely away from the sea.[3] ... I can never leave it again. It is an enchanted sea![4] ... Poor Guy—I feel I am with him only when near the sea.[5] ... I hear one calling me.[6] ... I must never more leave the sea.[7] ... he is still with me ... In the wistful ocean."[8]

Thus Martyn's young hero, like Ibsen's Stranger, may be looked upon as a kind of personification of the forces of Nature. "That man is like the sea."[9] In these words Ellida Wangel sums up the power of the Stranger. — "Is he not a genius of the sea?"[10] Lord Mask exclaims in sheer admiration for his young friend. The personification is enhanced by Mrs. Font's sinister remark that she looks upon the boy as "the imp of the sea fairie", whom she must get rid of, because in her opinion "those who belong to the sea, should go back to the sea".[11]

Although the last sentence has a very special meaning, it would be futile to deny that these words are but a verbal echo of Dr. Wangel's pleading with his own wife in *The Lady from the Sea*: "... the poor sick child must go to its own home again ... somewhere by the open sea—."[12] To make the connection even more

---

[1] *The Lady from the Sea*, Act II, p. 223.
[2] *An Enchanted Sea*, Act I, p. 131.
[3] *Ibid.*, Act III, p. 179.
[4] *Ibid.*, Act III, p. 180.
[5] *Ibid.*, Act IV, p. 192.
[6] *Ibid.*, Act IV, p. 193.
[7] *Ibid.*, Act IV, p. 193.
[8] *Ibid.*, Act IV, p. 194.
[9] *The Lady from the Sea*, Act III, p. 273.
[10] *An Enchanted Sea*, Act I, p. 133.
[11] *Ibid.*, Act I, p. 152.
[12] *The Lady from the Sea*, Act II, p. 224.

74

convincing one might quote the scene in which Dr. Wangel confides to his friend that "Ellida belongs to the sea-folk. ... Have you
not noticed that the people who live out by the open sea are like
a race apart? They seem almost to live the life of the sea itself."[1] ...
Finally, "Ellida wants to go home again; home to the sea."[2]

There are also some interesting parallels between Guy Font and
Ibsen's "little stranger-boy" Eyolf. The correspondence, however,
is mainly technical and had better be dealt with in the following
section.

Summing up, one might say that the character drawing of Martyn's drama clearly reveals the author's indebtedness to Ibsen.
Although the main action of *An Enchanted Sea* has comparatively
little in common with *The Lady from the Sea*, the fact remains that
Martyn's principal characters are both conceived and interpreted
in terms that point to Ibsen's "beautiful prose poem drama" of the
sea and the fascination it exerts upon the human soul.

Technique

The present investigation has already drawn attention to Mar-
tyn's indebtedness to Ibsen from the point of view of scenic method.
In this respect *An Enchanted Sea* is a case in point. To begin with,
Martyn's drama has a strong balladic atmosphere which is clearly
reminiscent of some of the plays of the Norwegian master, notably
The Lady from the Sea.

Let us consider for a moment the way in which the Irish dramatist introduces the story about the mermaid. In the very opening
pages the reader learns all about the strange marriage that took
place long ago between the first Lord Mask and the sea fairie. As
told above she soon feels imprisoned at the castle and longs to go

---

[1] *The Lady from the Sea*, Act IV, p. 288.
[2] *Ibid.*, Act IV, p. 311.

back to the sea. This turns out to be the dilemma of the present Lord Mask who also pines away at his home because it is "too inland" and he must be near the sea.

If the reader now turns to *The Lady from the Sea* he will be surprised to find exactly the same method of exposition. As a matter of fact the very first scene offers a striking parallel to Martyn's use of the sea fairie. For here we are confronted with the artist Ballested who is busy painting a picture which he intends to call "The Mermaid's End". This is his own description of the work:

> "By the rock in the foreground here, I mean to have a half-dead mermaid lying. ... She has strayed in from the sea, and can't find her way out again. So she lies here dying by inches in the brackish waters, you understand."[1]

Thus, in both plays, the story about the mermaid is introduced in order to symbolize the fate of one of the main characters.

Speaking about symbolism, it is interesting to observe that Martyn, as previously in *Maeve*, adopts Ibsen's habit, when one of his characters is attracted by another, of making the latter symbolic. Brand—Gerd (the Ice Church); Ellida Wangel—the Stranger (the Sea); Solness—Hilde (Youth); Eyolf—the Rat Wife (Death).

The Irish playwright, it will be remembered, follows a similar pattern in his drama of the sea. Both Lord Mask and Guy Font are irresistibly drawn to the sea fairie and Death. Mrs. Font's words: "The sea fairie is waiting to take him"[2] (Lord Mask) are but an echo of Allmer's remark in *Little Eyolf* about his son and the Rat Wife: "She has drawn him down into the depths—that you may be sure of, dear."[3]

Furthermore, Martyn's "white lady" who appears at Mask Castle to foretell the death of the last owner is used symbolically in a way that comes very close to Ibsen's treatment of the "white horses" of *Rosmersholm*. In this play, too, the "ghosts of the manor" appear whenever someone of the family is going to die.

It is also worthy of note that in both plays indomitable natural forces are at work. In *Rosmersholm* the fatal mill-stream, whose

---

[1] *The Lady from the Sea*, Act I, p. 170.
[2] *An Enchanted Sea*, Act IV, p. 202.
[3] *Little Eyolf*, Act II, p. 67.

roaring waters are heard in the distance throughout the action, has all the grandeur of a natural force which relentlessly sucks down the inhabitants of Rosmersholm, exactly as the sea does with some of the characters in *An Enchanted Sea*. Thus both plays are instinct with the same atmosphere of inevitability, brought about by the power of Nature and accentuated by visions, signs and portents of impending doom.

There are many other technical links between the master and the pupil. At the beginning of *An Enchanted Sea* the Irish playwright uses one of Ibsen's favourite tricks in order to prevent too rapid an exposition, namely a sudden break in the action. By skilfully interrupting the dialogue at a vital point, for instance when a secret is about to be disclosed, Ibsen manages to invest his plays with an atmosphere of suspense which is particularly important in his later works to conceal their lack of outward action.

In Martyn's drama the same device is put to effective use in the very opening scene which immediately strikes the right note of suspense.

YELVERTON. But why should they say he will be the last Lord Mask?
AGNES (*hesitatingly*). Because—well, because the tradition is that this sea fairie went back to the sea, and was never heard of again.
YELVERTON. Oh—they think she has now reappeared to—
AGNES. What steamer is that just come round the point?[1]

Turning to *The Lady from the Sea*, it is rather amusing to find that the third act has a similar interruption, caused by a steamer.

ELLIDA. Oh, I feel so thoroughly well. I feel so unspeakably happy! So safe! So safe— (*Looks out to the left.*) What large steamer is that coming in?[2]

Contemporary critics seem to have been puzzled by the character of Guy Font. One of them, Frank Fay, went to the length of asserting that Martyn should never have drawn the portrait of the little boy at all "because, after all, a play ought to be capable of being acted, and this character is almost impossible of realisation."[3]

---

[1] *An Enchanted Sea*, Act I, pp. 126–127.
[2] *The Lady from the Sea*, Act III, p. 253.
[3] *United Irishman*, November 4, 1904, quoted Sister Marie-Thérèse Courtney, *Edward Martyn and the Irish Theatre* (New York 1956), p. 96.

Personally I find this piece of criticism grotesquely wide of the mark. For Guy is the very pivot of the play. Without him the author might just as well have given up the whole project of writing *An Enchanted Sea*. But I think Martyn had a special reason for making a child the prime mover of his play. With Ibsen at his finger-tips, the Irish dramatist must have been struck by the frequency with which children appear in the works of his great forerunner. This is not the place to deal with them all. Suffice it to mention only two, the girl Hedvig in *The Wild Duck* and the young boy who lent his name to one of Ibsen's last dramas, i.e. *Little Eyolf*. It is significant that in both these plays a child acts as the pivot of the plot.[1]

Looking at Martyn's young hero from a technical point of view, I feel convinced that Ibsen's effective use of the child as centre of the action must have been an irresistible inducement to the Irish playwright to try his hand at a similar task. For Guy Font too, is the mainspring of the dramatic machinery. Like Eyolf he is fascinated by the supernatural. Ibsen's Rat Wife, who draws little Eyolf into the depths, reappears in Martyn's play in the shape of the sea fairie who is instrumental in bringing Guy Font to an untimely end in the waves of the sea.

As in Ibsen's drama, the tragedy occurs at an early stage. But the boys are stronger than death. From their watery graves both Eyolf and Guy keep haunting the other members of the house. Here is a passage in *Little Eyolf*:

ASTA ... Oh, my dear Alfred—let them rest—those who are gone. ...
ALLMERS — Yes, let them rest. (*Wringing his hands.*) But those who are gone—it is they that won't let us rest, Asta. Neither day nor night[2]

In *An Enchanted Sea* the death of Guy Font draws the following comment from Mrs. Font's daughter:

And so in death he is stronger for us than in life.[3]

---

[1] The present author saw *The Wild Duck* and *Little Eyolf* during the Ibsen Festival in Oslo 1956. The competent interpretation of the extremely difficult parts of the two children would, I think, have surprised Frank Fay, had he been there, and made him less inclined to look upon the character of Guy Font as being "almost impossible of realisation".

[2] *Little Eyolf*, Act II, p. 81.

[3] *An Enchanted Sea*, Act IV, p. 195.

Thus Martyn's young hero may be said to dominate the scene in practically the same way as the character of little Eyolf.

Finally, it is worth observing that *An Enchanted Sea* ends on a note of dramatic irony that the reader of, say, *The Wild Duck* or *Hedda Gabler* immediately recognizes as typically Ibsenian. The Irish dramatist prepares his readers for the death of Mrs. Font in much the same way as Ibsen does in dealing with the suicide of Hedda Gabler. Thus the fatal swing that ironically turns into a gibbet towards the end of Martyn's drama is hinted at throughout the action in a manner that closely resembles Ibsen's treatment of the pistol with which Hedda Gabler kills herself when the game is up.

These are the main parallels between the plays under discussion. The haunting power of *The Lady from the Sea* took possession of the Irish playwright. He found that he could use the sea atmosphere of Ibsen's drama for his own purpose. But in so doing, he added a new element, i.e. the legends of Manannan and Poseidon, the sea god of the Irish and Greek mythologies which are said to be akin.

Another difference between the two plays is to be found in Ibsen's famous retrospective technique. Much as he admired "the triumphant construction" of Ibsen's plays, the iron linking of the scenes and the gradual unravelling of the past, the Irish dramatist apparently did not even try to imitate this aspect of Ibsen's dramatic method in any of his own plays. None of them are constructed backwards like, for instance, *Ghosts*, *Rosmersholm* and, to some extent, *The Lady from the Sea*.[1]

Furthermore, Martyn does not share the Norwegian's predilection for the sententious phrase, which is quite in keeping with the didactic element of some of Ibsen's plays. *The Lady from the Sea*, for instance, ends with a kind of magic formula, i.e. "freedom under responsibility" which Martyn no doubt would have repudiated, just as it is repudiated by many modern critics. Unlike his great fore-

---

[1] A Norwegian authority on Ibsen points out that in his opinion the playwright's "principle of advancing through going backwards to revelations of the past is more than technique — it is the expression of his view of life, his profound belief in the importance of the past". (Francis Bull, *Ibsen. The Man and the Dramatist* (Oxford 1954), p. 12.

runner, the Irish dramatist does not want to ask questions or raise any problems. It is significant that Doctor Wangel's psychological cure of his wife in *The Lady from the Sea* did not suit Martyn and the lonely visionaries of his play "who have passed with their visions away". But in creating his own enchanted ocean, he could not resist the incantatory power of Ibsen's drama of the sea.

CHAPTER V

Grangecolman

There is an interval of exactly ten years between Edward Martyn's second volume of plays, containing *The Tale of a Town* and *An Enchanted Sea*, and the publication of *Grangecolman* in 1912. This drama was among the earliest productions of the Independent Theatre Company. It is a play of cold realism sometimes lapsing into melodrama.

Plot

Act I

Grangecolman is an ancient country seat near Dublin. The present owner, Michael Colman, originally belonged to the Quinns, a well-to-do family who always "held their heads high commercially". He became one of the Colmans of Grangecolman by marrying the heiress, an alliance that brought money into this branch of old Irish gentry. At the death of his wife, Colman, who is now a man of sixty, was left with only one daughter, Catharine, to look after the house. This young girl soon became engrossed with the feminist movement, training herself for a medical career. She is now married to Lucius Devlin, an incorrigible idler who once caught her fancy as an agitator for women's rights. Catharine fails, however, in the medical profession, partly because people "have no confidence in female doctors".

Let down by her husband, who goes on cherishing barren ideals instead of taking up a decent job, Catharine reluctantly finds that

they are both thrown upon her father's resources for their future
existence. Unwilling to accept the duties of her home, Catharine
brings Miss Clare Farquhar into the house to look after Colman
and help him to carry on his studies of heraldry and genealogy
which form his intellectual pastime. This turns out to be a successful arrangement as far as Colman and his young amanuensis are
concerned. They soon find happiness in their mutual work. Neg-
lected by his own daughter, Colman cannot help conceiving a
middle-aged passion for his responsive protégée.

On her return to Grangecolman, Catharine is struck by the
friendly atmosphere of the home that used to be a prison to her.
But very soon she becomes aware of Colman's true feelings for
Miss Farquhar. Finding herself supplanted in the life of her father
by his secretary, Catharine immediately sets about to put an end
to this unexpected love-affair. She persuades her father that she is
beginning to take an interest in his work. Her next step is to inform
Miss Farquhar that her services are no longer required. From now
on she herself is going to be Mr. Colman's secretary.

Act II

Catharine tells her husband that she has put an end to Miss
Farquhar's career. In vain does Lucius try to persuade his wife
that in dismissing the secretary she is only increasing Colman's
infatuation for the young girl. Catharine, however, tells her father
that he must choose between herself and Miss Farquhar whose
presence in the house is bound to bring misfortune to them all.
In order to frighten the superstitious old man into obedience
Catharine insinuates that she has already had "the usual warning"
from the white lady that haunts Grangecolman. As if to emphasize
her words, Horan, the butler, is heard outside the room crying for
help. He enters in a hurry telling everybody that he has just seen
the family ghost. Colman is very near total collapse when the
"ghost" suddenly materializes in the shape of Miss Farquhar dressed
in white for dinner. In an interview with the girl, Colman explains
to her that his nerves are unhinged because of the "dreadful tales
hanging about the old place". Feeling that he will be lost without

6 – 60113001 *Jan Setterquist*

Miss Farquhar, Colman makes bold to propose to the girl who is
only too happy to accept the hand of her "master". The act closes
on the couple announcing their union. Catharine stares at them as
if struck by lightning.

Act III

Colman's daughter is planning to prevent the marriage between
her father and Miss Farquhar. Left alone with the young girl,
Catharine suffers the humiliation of being openly denounced as a
failure. In a final effort to defeat her young opponent, Mrs. Devlin
resorts to a desperate scheme. Knowing that Miss Farquhar does
not believe in phantoms, Catharine decides to play the family ghost
in order to provoke her rival to fire at "the white lady of Grangecolman". Shortly afterwards a bullet from Miss Farquhar's revol-
ver puts a melodramatic end to the story as well as to the empty
life of Catharine Devlin.

Theme

In one of his books of travel J. M. Synge drew attention to a
dramatic theme that lay hidden in the Irish countryside waiting
for the competent explorer. "Everyone," he writes in *Wicklow*, "is
used in Ireland to the tragedy that is bound up with the lives of
farmers and fishing people." But, he adds, "if a playwright chose
to go through the Irish country houses he would find material, it is
likely, for many gloomy plays that would turn on the dying away
of these old families, and on the lives of the one or two delicate
girls that are left so often to represent a dozen hearty men who
were alive a generation or two ago."[1]

[1] J. M. Synge, *In Wicklow, West Kerry and Connemara* (Dublin 1911), pp.
52–53.

Synge's own literary activities, it is true, centred almost exclusively on folk drama. But some of Martyn's plays, notably *Grangecolman*, show that Synge was perfectly right in calling attention to the native material for domestic drama. On the other hand, it is extremely unlikely that Martyn's achievement in the field would have met with Synge's approval. The point is, however, that Martyn was bent on showing the possibilities of another kind of drama, a drama both Irish and cosmopolitan.

The main theme of *Grangecolman* is the socially maladjusted woman. It is a story of a *femme fatale* and the ruinous part she plays in the lives of other people. This theme is treated in a way that immediately invites comparison with the only misogynist play that Ibsen ever wrote—*Hedda Gabler*.

Character

A study of *Grangecolman* reveals certain interesting parallels between some of Martyn's characters and those of Ibsen. Thus Colman himself is partly traced on the figure of Rosmer in *Rosmersholm*. In both plays we are confronted with "the quiet student" who sits musing over his genealogical tables and historical collections, assisted only by an attractive young woman who has come to the old manor. They fall in love with each other. But the man is under the spell of the haunted house and their love is thwarted by "the family ghost".

Here the parallelism ends. Colman is something of an upstart, well aware of the power of money. Rosmer, on the other hand, is an idealist who wants to ennoble the minds of his countrymen. Besides, the Irish landowner is as reactionary in his social outlook as Rosmer, the aristocrat, is liberal.

Looking at the cast of Martyn's drama, Catharine Devlin is, however, the figure that most readily invites comparison with some of Ibsen's leading characters. Rebekka West and Hilde Wangel for

6* – 60113001

instance, with their innate love of power, will stop at nothing to
attain their end. The very fact that their road to success crosses the
threshold of another woman's home merely adds to the thrill of
the hunt.

One must, however, look elsewhere in order to find Martyn's
chief source of inspiration. For Catharine Devlin is no doubt
primarily modelled on Hedda Gabler, Ibsen's famous study of a
femme fatale. Not only do they share an all-absorbing passion for
dominating other people's lives. They also betray the same negative
attitude towards married life, finding compensation in a masculine
craving for action.

Unsatisfied by their partners, who both cut a poor figure, Hedda
Gabler as well as Catharine Devlin find a dangerous outlet for their
subdued passions. Soon the negative and the sterile that characterizes both heroines turns into sadism and the stage is set for the
cruel game of cat and mouse.

Hedda Gabler spoils the union between her former lover, a dissipated scholar, and his guardian angel, whereas Catharine Devlin
makes a desperate attempt to put an end to her father's pathetic
romance with a young girl who threatens to upset her plans.
Ibsen's heroine, like Martyn's, feels that life is slipping from her.
Little by little this same feeling of having lost their footing in life
begins to tell on their nerves so that in both plays the heroine is
clearly moving on the border of insanity.

Thus Hedda Gabler and Catharine Devlin are birds of a feather
in more than one way. They are both consumed by a desperate
passion for life, i.e. the free and beautiful life of their visions which
form such a striking contrast to their own dreary existence. Hampered by a sense of mental discomfort, they fail, however, to find
a positive outlet for their intellectual capacity.[1] Under these circumstances it is only natural that the enlightened lady doctor of Martyn's
play should hate being reduced to inactivity. A stranger to her own
family, Catharine Devlin, like Hedda Gabler, finds herself lost in
a social vacuum. The crisis is accentuated by the fact that both

---

[1] Hedda Gabler: "I often think there is only one thing in the world I have
any turn for. ... Boring myself to death." (Act II, pp. 81–82.) Cf. Catharine
Devlin's outburst: "I am hopeless and weary, and if this crowning injury comes
to me, I don't care what I do." (*Grangecolman*, Act II, p. 25.)

women are equally disappointed in their husbands who fail to live
up to their ideals. Having lost their illusions of a carefree independent life, both heroines are entirely thrown upon their own
resources in their revolt against the outer world, a world that could
not possibly be less congenial to their temperament.

In this heavy atmosphere the morbid and the destructive about
the two women gets the better of them. When all other roads seem
to be closed, that of the parasite is always left open. As their dreams
fail to materialize, both Hedda Gabler and Catharine Devlin seek
compensation in a desperate struggle for self-assertion. Frustrated
in their ambitions, the two heroines deliberately set about ruining
the lives of their competitors. For why should other people enjoy
a happiness that they themselves can never hope to find?

In each play the heroine is confronted with a rivalling woman
who falls an easy victim to the tricks of her relentless persecutor.
Thus we have on the one side Hedda Gabler's erotic devilries which
bring about the estrangement of a loving couple, on the other
Catharine Devlin's wicked designs on her own father and on the
woman he intends to marry. The parallel between the two plays is
emphasized by the fact that in the end Catharine Devlin, like Hedda
Gabler, falls in her own trap with death as the only possible solution.

Ibsen's heroine, like Martyn's, behaves exactly like the dog in
the manger. They both hate other women, especially those who
find happiness in love. For love is a word that none of them seems
able to understand or even let pass over their lips. Their dilemma
is that of the unemployed wife trying to escape the monotony of an
unsuccessful marriage. Everything that is important to Hedda and
Catharine comes to nothing. Ibsen's neurotic heroine speaks of the
ridiculous and the sordid lying like a curse on everything she
touches.[1] Catharine Devlin, thwarted and tortured beyond endur-
ance, rails at her father in the following outburst: "Oh! Will no one
understand? Don't you see that nothing would really have mattered
if things I had set my heart on had only prospered with me."[2]

Like Hedda Gabler, Martyn's heroine looks upon life with the
eyes of an aesthete unable to endure the plebeian manners of her

---

[1] *Hedda Gabler*, Act IV, p. 176.
[2] *Grangecolman*, Act II, p. 26.

fellow-creatures. "Yes, I've been a great enthusiast. There is no one who has had such enthusiasm for what is lofty and great and beautiful in life as I. I am proud of it, and also of my contempt for the sort of wisdom of such as you."[1]

As stated above neither the eccentric visions of Hedda Gabler nor the beautiful though self-centred dreams of Catharine Devlin come true and evil and hatred has the last word. Thus the inadequacy of a narrow aesthetic outlook on life is demonstrated along much the same lines in both plays. And yet it is equally clear that this very vision, this glimpse of beauty and happiness, inspires the reader with a certain amount of pity for the two heroines who otherwise would have appeared merely morbid and destructive.

Furthermore, it is significant that both heroines confess to having overestimated the intellectual capacity of their partners. Witness the following conversation:

HEDDA. I see no reason why he should not one day come to the front, after all.

BRACK (*looks at her hesitatingly*). I thought that you, like every one else, expected him to attain the highest distinction.

HEDDA (*with an expression of fatigue*). Yes, so I did.[2]

Turning to Martyn, the corresponding passage runs as follows:

CATHARINE — What matter what he did or didn't, when he didn't do the real thing.

COLMAN. You mean what you expected of him. Ah, you thought him a much greater man than he was, Catharine.

CATHARINE. I did. ... Besides his University course was so brilliant.[3]

Hedda Gabler refuses to accept the fact that she has been supplanted in the love of her rejected admirer by another woman strong enough to offer resistance. Furthermore, she will not tolerate her rival's attempt at reclaiming the dissipated scholar as she herself wishes "to have power to mould a human destiny".[4] In a similar way Catharine Devlin finds herself superseded in the affections of her father by another woman. Like Hedda, Martyn's heroine

---

[1] *Grangecolman*, Act III, p. 37.
[2] *Hedda Gabler*, Act II, pp. 69–70.
[3] *Grangecolman*, Act I, pp. 7–8.
[4] *Hedda Gabler*, Act II, p. 114.

starts intriguing in order to spoil her rival's love romance. Like Hedda, she is finally caught in her own trap.

CATHARINE. All I know is that real life has somehow got near to me at last, and (*vehemently*) that I loathe it.[1]

With this should be compared Hedda Gabler's outburst towards the end of the drama:

HEDDA (*looks up—with an expression of loathing*). That too! Oh, what curse is it that makes everything I touch turn ludicrous and mean?[2]

Thus the embarrassing position of Hedda and Catharine is gradually exposed until at the end of the two plays the tormented souls of the heroines cry out in utter loneliness. Feeling nothing but disgust for life, both Hedda and Catharine find peace in death which seems to offer them the final morbid thrill.

Technique

Grangecolman may be looked upon as a final example of Martyn's careful adaptation of some of Ibsen's most characteristic technical devices.

The very setting of the Irishman's play strikes a typical Ibsenian note. For the scene of the action is a lonely old country seat haunted by a family ghost. Although the supernatural element is introduced by the Irish dramatist in a crude, melodramatic manner, it is hard not to think of *Rosmersholm*, to say nothing about *Ghosts*, as a possible source of inspiration. As a matter of fact, Martyn was particularly fond of *Rosmersholm* which he looked upon as "one of the master's finest and most absorbing studies in psychological action. ... The old Norwegian country house which gives its name to the tragedy fills the background with its ghostly, still life".[3]

---

[1] *Grangecolman*, Act III, p. 41.
[2] *Hedda Gabler*, Act IV, p. 176.
[3] Martyn papers, quoted Denis Gwynn, *op. cit.*, pp. 147–148.

88

Examining the stage directions of *Grangecolman*, we find that
they simply abound in minute observations of a kind that immediately recalls Ibsen's novelizing method of introducing his characters to the reading public by way of visual suggestion. There is also
the same tendency of stressing the relationship between a person's
outward appearance and his character. To take only one example,
this is how Catharine Devlin's husband is presented:

> "He is a tall, slightly built man, with marked and rather delicate
> features, hair rather long, an untrimmed beard, and spectacles. His
> clothes are ill-fitting, and his coat buttoned up to the throat suggests
> a person careful of himself. He is about thirty-five years of age."[1]

One of Ibsen's favourite technical inventions, originating no
doubt from Scribe and the well-made play, is the habit of making
his characters indulge in some kind of game that sums up the
situation[2] while at the same time throwing the main plot into relief.
A typical instance of the same technique is to be found in the last
act of *Grangecolman:*

> MISS FARQUHAR. I must play, or else I shall feel gloomy.
> LUCIUS. Why not let us have a game of billiards? You beat me last
> time.
> MISS FARQUHAR. Very well. I will now give you your revenge.
> CATHARINE (*significantly*). Revenge is a dangerous word, Miss Farquhar.[3]

Even a brief examination of the stage-properties of *Grangecolman*
reveals Martyn's indebtedness to Ibsen. Thus the reader is at once
struck by the fact that a couple of revolvers form part of the plot
in much the same way as General Gabler's pistols in *Hedda Gabler*.
The Norwegian heroine's carefree handling of the dangerous weapon immediately suggests her *noli me tangere* attitude towards life
and even led a critic to the ridiculous assumption that Hedda Gabler
herself is, in fact, a pistol.[4]

Not only does the theme of the fatal fire-arms appear in both
plays with the frequency of a *leitmotif*. Far more revealing is the

---

[1] *Grangecolman*, Act I, p. 9.
[2] See e.g. *Catilina, Lady Inger, The Warriors of Helgeland, The Pretenders,
The League of Youth, A Doll's House*, and *The Wild Duck*.
[3] *Grangecolman*, Act III, p. 39.
[4] Jennette Lee, *The Ibsen Secret* (New York 1907), pp. 26–27.

fact that Martyn follows Ibsen's method of introducing the theme
at the very beginning of the drama to create an uncanny atmosphere
and to prepare the reader for the final catastrophe. Thus there is
a strong link between the first act of both plays and the last where
death comes for the heroine who is silenced for ever by a bullet
from the family pistol.

Considering for a moment Martyn's treatment of the landscape
which played such a significant part in his earlier dramas, there is
no denying the fact that the atmosphere of *Grangecolman* has much
in common with the spirit of gloom that pervades some of Ibsen's
finest plays. It is, I think, hardly a coincidence that the autumnal
setting of *Hedda Gabler*, so congenial to a drama that deals with
the decline and fall of a *femme fatale*, should have tempted Martyn
to create a similar background of "the yellow leaf" for his own
tragedy.

Once again, though with less skill, the Irish dramatist adopted
Ibsen's clever habit of dragging in the landscape both by visual
suggestion and by means of dialogue in which the scenery is brought
to bear on the different characters of the play. A single example
will illustrate this. In the first act of *Hedda Gabler* the heroine is
caught unaware by her husband in a scene that gives an early
glimpse of Hedda's true state of mind.

HEDDA (*walks about the room, raising her arms and clenching her hands
as if in desperation. Then she flings back the curtains from the glass door,
and stands there looking out. Presently* TESMAN *returns and closes the door
behind him*).
TESMAN ... What are you looking at, Hedda?
HEDDA (*once more calm and mistress of herself*). I am looking at the
leaves. They are so yellow—so withered.
TESMAN ... Well, you see, we are well into September now.
HEDDA (*again restless*). Yes, to think of it!—Already in—in September.[1]

Turning to *Grangecolman*, one need not study the play for long
to notice the same romantic convention of relating the emotional
life of the main characters to the surrounding landscape. As with
Ibsen, illustrative action and dialogue combine to produce a vivid
effect that sticks in the mind. This, for instance, is Martyn's
heroine at the cross-roads:

[1] *Hedda Gabler*, Act I, p. 25.

90

90

CATHARINE (*Goes to window at left and draws back the curtains. The moon shines in*). What a clear, beautiful night. (*Dreamily.*) Those hectic tints of autumn have faded under the frosty moon to a whiteness of death.

MISS FARQUHAR (*with awe*). Yes. How cold it looks outside.

CATHARINE. How peaceful to the heart that longs for rest.

MISS FARQUHAR. The trees—the lawn are frightfully still.

CATHARINE (*unfastening the window*). Come, let us walk out.

MISS FARQUHAR (*shrinks*). Oh, no. I couldn't bear it.

CATHARINE. Why couldn't you bear it?

MISS FARQUHAR (*shuddering*). I don't know. Your words—There is something ghastly about the whiteness of the night.[1]

In the light of what has already been said about Martyn's treatment of the landscape in his earlier plays, the above analysis seems to confirm the impression that Irish scenery was hardly the author's sole source of inspiration.

Furthermore, Martyn's close reliance upon Ibsen's scenic method is evidenced by the fact that *Grangecolman* is a highly selective drama. From plays like *Ghosts*, *Rosmersholm* and *Hedda Gabler* the Irish dramatist learned that a true tragedy had better not be stifled by an excessive number of actors. Like Ibsen's plays, *Grangecolman* passes as nearly as possible in solitude. Surrounded by only a handful of characters, Martyn's heroine, like Hedda Gabler, stands head and shoulders above the people around her.

Another technical peculiarity that links Martyn's drama with that of Ibsen is the tendency to reduce external action to a minimum in order to focus the reader's attention upon the inner drama, i.e. the drama of the human soul at a crisis. In *Hedda Gabler*, as well as in *Grangecolman*, we receive the heroine ripe for her undoing. For Martyn, like Ibsen, is mainly concerned with writing what may conveniently be called the fifth act of the drama.

It needs stressing that in both plays retribution is coming not from without but from within. *Grangecolman*, like *Hedda Gabler*, is the story of the biter bit. But, and this is an important difference between the two plays, Ibsen's heroine is a good loser. Her head proudly erect, Hedda Gabler turns away from "the banquet of life", to use her own high-flown expression. Catharine Devlin, on

---

[1] *Grangecolman*, Act III, pp. 36–37.

the other hand, merely adds to her register of sins by courting death in a way that ruins the lives of her own father and the woman he loves. Besides, in killing his heroine in full view of the audience, Martyn committed a crudity that would have shocked the author of *Hedda Gabler*.

As the previous discussion has shown, Martyn was a great admirer of *Rosmersholm*. From a technical point of view the author's indebtedness to this particular drama is evidenced in more than one way. At the very beginning of *Grangecolman* the intimacy between Colman and the young girl is suddenly exposed to Catharine as her father calls Miss Farquhar by her Christian name. This scene is evidently traced on a similar episode in *Rosmersholm* where Rosmer's love for Rebekka is hinted at in precisely the same way.[1]

Another technical resemblance between the two plays is the way in which the supernatural element that dominates both *Rosmersholm* and *Grangecolman* is given a realistic motivation. Thus Rebekka's white shawl and Miss Farquhar's white dinner dress serve the same purpose of providing a logical explanation of the ghostly disturbances at the two lonely country-houses.

What places *Grangecolman*, as compared with *Rosmersholm* and *Hedda Gabler*, on an altogether lower artistic level is precisely the sum of the Irishman's shortcomings as a playwright. These have already been dealt with in the above analysis and need not be enumerated again. It is to be regretted that in telling his story Martyn did not observe the great objectivity of the old master. No verdict is passed upon Rebekka West, nor on Hedda Gabler, whose complicated character and tragic fate cannot fail to stir our imagination.

The finely conceived portrait of Catharine Devlin on the other hand is unfortunately marred by Martyn's misogyny which at the end of the drama becomes so exaggerated as to rob the heroine of all human proportions. Whatever the author's intention, the fact remains that the desperate woman who welcomes death from her own pistol seems no more real than the phantoms which are said to haunt Grangecolman.

However, even in this play there is, as we have seen, more than one indication that Martyn tried to adopt Ibsen's method of com-

---

[1] *Grangecolman*, Act I, p. 6. *Rosmersholm*, Act II, p. 62.

bining realism with poetry. But the Irishman's bias and lack of inspiration were too obvious for such efforts ever to be rewarded. That is why, in spite of the author's ambition, the heroine of *Grangecolman* remains a Hedda Gabler in miniature.

In *Rosmersholm*, as in most of Ibsen's plays, there is an ethical background, a constant questioning of current morality of which there is practically no evidence in the theatre of Edward Martyn. The Irish playwright does not want to "teach or prove anything", to quote a few words from J. M. Synge's attack upon the Northern master. Above all, being a devout Catholic, Martyn looks upon morality as something fixed once and for all, something that is not to be questioned, least of all in a work for the theatre.

And yet, when all is said there is no denying the fact that *Grangecolman* is of great interest to the student of the Literary Revival as a noteworthy attempt to introduce a new kind of drama, a drama both Irish and cosmopolitan. Of the three Irishmen behind the famous manifesto, quoted above, no one came closer than Edward Martyn to the gallant slogan of the Irish Literary Theatre: "Everywhere critics and writers, who wish for something better than the ordinary play of commerce, turn to Norway for an example and an inspiration."

CHAPTER VI

Conclusion

With the publication of the present study I have brought the first part of my investigation of Ibsen's influence upon the early Anglo-Irish drama to an end. To illustrate my thesis, I have chosen two dramatists who do not seem to have anything in common apart from the fact that they happened to belong to the same movement. The one, J. M. Synge, concealed his own indebtedness to Ibsen by making negative pronouncements on the works of the great Norwegian, the other, Edward Martyn, proved a devout Ibsenite both as playwright and dramatic critic.

Happily, we have Synge's own words for the fact that he had actually read and pondered Ibsen's dramas. In the preface to *The Tinker's Wedding*, the Irish writer takes stand against the dramaturgy of the Northern master. "The drama, like the symphony, does not teach or prove anything. Analysts with their problems, and teachers with their systems, are soon as old-fashioned as the pharmacopœia of Galen—look at Ibsen and the Germans—but the best plays of Ben Jonson and Molière can no more go out of fashion than the blackberries on the hedges."

The drama, Synge goes on to say, needs humour. That seems to be his quarrel with Ibsen. In the preface to *The Playboy*, Synge accuses the Norwegian playwright of "dealing with the reality of life in joyless and pallid words. On the stage one must have reality, and one must have joy; and that is why the intellectual modern drama has failed." In other words, Ibsen is too serious to satisfy a man like Synge. Such an objection which, incidentally, covers only part of the old master's literary achievement, is rather surprising on the part of the author of that poignant little tragedy, *Riders to the Sea*, published only a few years earlier. However, the arrogant note of Synge's attack is in itself an indirect proof of the fact that Ibsen occupied his thoughts more than he cared to admit, even to himself.

Although the Irish playwright stresses his belief that the drama must be humourous and full of laughter, he does not, I think, intend to suggest that these qualities would of themselves exclude the problem from the drama. The spirit of his own plays bears ample witness to the veracity of this statement. As a matter of fact, nearly all Synge's dramas offer an interesting problem presented in a form that agrees with the author's ideas of the humourous twist of mind and the poetic language of the Irish people.

In the Shadow of the Glen treats of a theme that is well known from many folktales: the old man who feigns death in order to put his young wife's fidelity to the test. The heroine of the play, Nora, has a feeling of being buried alive "in the shadow of the glen". Driven by her longing for a dimly-perceived horizon, the young woman forsakes her home out of her own free will. In other words, Nora prefers the hazards of the future to the kind of conjugal hide-and-seek that embitters her life.

Apart from the fact that the social background of the Irishman's play is utterly unlike that of the works of Ibsen, there is more than one connecting link between Synge's Nora and her Norwegian namesake in *A Doll's House*. Both plays introduce us to an ill-assorted couple whose union is spoilt by a bullying husband who does not allow his wife any kind of private life. Furthermore, it is worth observing that in either drama the final exposure of the heroine is followed by a great *scène à faire*, ending up with the woman banging the door on her husband. The inconclusive ending is another characteristic of the two plays under comparison. Both dramas close with a question-mark. If Synge had been asked, as Ibsen actually was, what became of Nora, he might well have subscribed to the old master's opinion that he regarded the future of the heroine as a side-issue.

Synge's Nora is also partly modelled on another character in Ibsen's famous gallery of remarkable women, i.e. Ellida Wangel in *The Lady from the Sea*. She, too, has sold herself to her husband. Her marriage, like Nora's, has proved a blind alley until one day both women are suddenly called back to real life by a stranger who is only too willing to open up the new horizon for which their pent-up souls are yearning.

True to his artistic creed, Synge carefully refrains from pointing the moral of the play. Ibsen, on the other hand, for all his ambition to stand aloof from his characters, often suffers from an over-scrupulous conscience that accounts for the author's predilection for the literary sermon. In this respect there is a marked difference between the two writers. Synge, it is true, based his first play on a plot of native origin. But the genuine Irish twist of *In the Shadow of the Glen* must not blind us to the fact that the play gives clear indication of being a variation of the well-known theme of *A Doll's House*.

Synge's second drama, *Riders to the Sea*, deals with the most vital problem of the inhabitants of the Aran Islands, i.e. the inexorable forces of Nature. The subject was no doubt inspired by the Irishman's island experience. But the development of the main theme reveals Synge's indebtedness to the author of *The Lady from the Sea*. In this play, too, the incantatory power of the sea, which frightens and allures, repels and attracts its victims, is felt as a hidden undercurrent throughout the action. The evocative description of the sea and the perilous attraction it exerts upon the human soul is not, however, the only element in *Riders to the Sea* to invite comparison with the Ibsenian theatre. The suggestive vision of the horses that figure in the title of the play, as well as the interpretation of the dreadful sight as a portent of death, can be traced back to *Rosmersholm*. In this drama the "ghosts of the manor" are two white horses which appear whenever someone in the house of Rosmer is going to die. Similarly, Synge uses the *motif* of the horses to presage the catastrophe. In *Rosmersholm* there is furthermore the fatal mill-race which has all the grandeur of a natural force taking as its prey first one, then another member of the family, exactly as the sea does in *Riders to the Sea*. Most revealing, perhaps, is the scene in which the sinister truth comes home to the old mother in *Riders to the Sea* in precisely the same way as the shadow of the past begins to haunt Osvald's mother in the famous "ghost scene" that ends the first act of *Ghosts*.

The Tinker's Wedding is less rewarding from the point of view of Ibsenian influence. Yet, the very spirit of this play has something in common with the atmosphere of *The League of Youth*. Man is more or less at the mercy of chance. Mounted on Love's own merry-go-round, the persons of the play change partners as readily as a pair of shoes. This general note of "match-making" that characterizes *The League of Youth* constitutes the nearest approach to Synge's wilful little farce. But on the whole, we had better speak only of possible impressions rather than of actual influence from Ibsen's drama.

The Well of the Saints is concerned with people who live in an imaginary world of illusions which they jealously guard against the intrusion of reality. The author stresses his belief that the "life-lie" is indispensable to man's happiness and that a sudden disenchantment must of necessity spell disaster. Thus Synge's drama has much in common with *The Wild Duck* whose main conflict centres on precisely the same problem. Both plays discuss the question of blindness, physical as well as spiritual. Like Hjalmar Ekdal, Synge's blind couple are born escapists who readily indulge in day-dreams which cannot possibly be reconciled to naked facts. When, through the gratuitous meddling of an outsider, the scales are removed from their eyes, Synge's beggars suffer the shock of being suddenly thrown out into a world without mercy. But before we lose sight of them they are once more comfortably ensconced in their imaginary kingdom. In other words, Synge arrives at exactly the same conclusion as Ibsen. Both writers consider illusion and self-deception to be far more important to the success of certain people than a disillusioned recognition of the truth. Says Relling in *The Wild Duck*: "Rob the average man of his life-lie, and you rob him of his happiness at the same stroke."

Synge's best known work, *The Playboy of the Western World*, is based on an actual occurrence recorded in his travel-sketches *The Aran Islands*. However, a close study of Synge's drama and its possible sources reveals the interesting fact that the hero of the play, Christy Mahon, has much in common with Ibsen's famous playboy, Peer Gynt, to say nothing of another day-dreamer, Hjalmar Ekdal in *The Wild Duck*. Both Peer and Christy are braggarts and boisterous good-for-nothings blessed with a vivid imagination and a youthful charm which make them irresistible to women. If a girl takes them seriously, they are at once ready to confess their love for her in the most highflown language. But a romantic strain and a habit of transforming the dreary truths of their everyday life into brilliant and colourful lies are by no means the only qualities shared by Christy and Peer Gynt. At times both country lads are able to take a realistic view of life. Ibsen's hero, like Synge's, soon discovers that he can use his grip on other people to feather his own nest. Starting with two empty hands, Peer Gynt rises to become a ship-owner on a large scale. In a similar way Christy turns out to be something of a social-climber, marching straight into the heart of the heroine on his way to a carefree existence ever after.

Synge, it is true, was no "Playboy". Nor was Ibsen a Peer Gynt. Both dramatists were readers and observers, rather than men of action. But this would not prevent either of them from feeling akin to his hero. The point is, however, that the juxtaposition of the two plays clearly shows that the Irishman's treatment of the original story of *The Playboy* was conditioned by his impressions of *Peer Gynt*. In Ibsen's hero, with his sudden changes of mood, his chameleon-like accomodation to circumstances, as well as his excitability and incapacity to distinguish between right and wrong, fact and fancy, Synge must certainly have recognized the playboy of his own drama.

Thus we are once more reminded of the fact that the Irishman's denunciation of Ibsen does not entitle us to question *any* connection between the two writers. This view is confirmed by a recent statement by a well-known Norwegian authority on Ibsen. "The progeny of Peer Gynt and Hjalmar Ekdal", Bull writes, "is very numerous, and may often be found in precisely those plays whose authors have most ostentatiously proclaimed revolt against the Ibsenian theatre."[1]

Peer Gynt, however, is not the only Ibsen drama that may have influenced the author of *The Playboy*. The possessive manner in which Pegeen chooses Christy for her hero as well as her constant prompting of the young man to beat his own record, is, I think, strongly reminiscent of Hilde Wangel's bold game with Solness the Master Builder. Most striking, perhaps, is the parallel treatment of the final scene where the hero is suddenly dethroned leaving the young woman to pour out her lonely heart at the loss of her love. Hilde's almost maniacal cry *"My—my* Master Builder!"" when the death of Solness puts her scheming to an abrupt end, is echoed

---

[1] Bull, *op. cit.*, p. 15.

exactly in the "wild lamentations" of Synge's heroine: "Oh, my grief, I've lost him surely. I've lost the only Playboy of the Western World."

Synge's last drama, *Deirdre of the Sorrows*, which he never quite finished, is of less interest in this connection. But the main conflict no doubt resembles that of *Love's Comedy*. Both plays treat of a love that demands all or nothing. There is also the same fear of the decay of love. Finally, Synge's heroine, like Ibsen's, is forced to admit that only by renouncing her love while it is still triumphant can she conquer time and immortalize her beautiful dream.

The present analysis seems to me to warrant the conclusion that there is an undeniable affinity between Ibsen's dramas and those of Synge, plainly indicated in the points of resemblance cited above. The juxtaposition of Synge's plays with those of Ibsen reveals an indubitable correlation of theme, character drawing and technique.

This similarity, however, does not in any way detract from the literary distinction of the Irish playwright. The proof of Synge's originality lies in the fact that the Ibsenian influence was never permitted to efface the genuine Irishness of his literary profile. That this is so, is best shown by the fact that so many scholars have been able to read Synge without observing his indebtedness to Ibsen.

On the other hand, Synge's criticism of Ibsen's drama makes it possible for the reader to discover the main points of divergence between the two dramatists, showing how Synge with his insistence on "joy" and "humour" finds matter for a completely amoral comedy, or tragi-comedy, in a subject already treated by Ibsen, the ethicist and moralist, as a tragedy. But the negative attitude displayed by Synge towards the great innovator of the modern drama can no longer conceal the fact that, generally speaking, the Irish playwright may be said to take interest in situations that involve the same questions as those dealt with by his Norwegian forerunner. He also maps out these problems in much the same way, and the conclusions, if any, are those already arrived at by Ibsen.

Thus Synge himself bears ample witness to the validity of his own artistic creed, as expressed in the preface to *The Playboy*: "All art is a collaboration."

In 1917 Ernest A. Boyd wrote as follows: "There is felt to be an increasing need for a theatre in Ireland which will hold up to nature that half of the mirror which is not visible in the Irish National Theatre, where a too exclusive care for the folk-drama has resulted in giving a one-sided appearance to our dramatic activities."[1]

This is where Edward Martyn comes in as a champion of Ibsen and the continental drama. *The Heather Field* and *Maeve*, by far the most successful of Martyn's plays, represent a new departure in the history of Ireland's Literary Revival. For here we have a deliberate attempt to adopt some of the great Norwegian's fundamental principles for the creation of drama. Unlike most Ibsenites of the time, who saw only the social reformer, not the lyric visionary, the Irish dramatist instinctively sided with Ibsen the poet.

In *The Heather Field* and *Maeve*, where "human emotion is the whole of the play," Martyn did indeed approach the high mountains of his great master. But his imagination never soared to such heights in any of the remaining plays which are all marked by a gradual decline. Though less convincing from the point of view of literary workmanship, these plays are nevertheless of great interest to the scholar as an evidence of Martyn's dogged fight for an Irish drama independent of the folk-play.

With the passing of the years, however, Martyn's drama takes on a new aspect. Although still faithful to Ibsen, the Irish playwright tends to abandon his early highly poetic themes in order to concentrate his efforts on various topics of everyday life. *The Tale of a Town*, for instance, is a case in point. The play, it is true, falls flat by the side of *An Enemy of the People* that inspired it. Yet Martyn's drama is not dwarfed into insignificance, for here again the author was breaking fresh ground.

Even in plays with a legendary background, such as *Maeve* and *An Enchanted Sea*, the native element of the story cannot conceal the fact that the strains were caught up from Ibsen who left his mark not only on the main conflict and on some of the leading characters but also on the technique of the Irishman's drama.

It is characteristic of Martyn's way of working that most of his plays include elements from more than one of Ibsen's works.

---

[1] Boyd, *op. cit.*, p. 30.

Grangecolman forms no exception to the rule. The heroine of the drama is clearly modelled on Hedda Gabler, whereas the idea of making a haunted old country-house the centre of the action may be traced back to *Ghosts* and *Rosmersholm*. Looking for new directions, the Irish dramatist once more sought and found inspiration in Ibsen. *Grangecolman* is not a great play. But it holds its own by the side of Martyn's other plays as an interesting attempt to enrich the repertory of the contemporary Irish stage.

Martyn's indebtedness to Ibsen does not, however, exclude certain points of divergence between the two dramatists. Some of these are undoubtedly due to a fundamental difference of character and temperament. Unlike Ibsen, the Irish playwright does not want to raise any problems or question current morality. Dramatic didacticism was not for him.[1] This is quite in keeping with the author's religious considerations which made him shun the daring problems that Ibsen tackled in play after play. It is, I think, something of a paradox that Martyn, the devout Catholic, should have found his way to Ibsen, the Protestant. The author of *Ave* was right—"the drama brings strange fowls to roost".

Equally conspicuous is the Irishman's lack of humour, as well as his negative attitude to nearly all the women of his plays, with Maeve as the one notable exception.

Then there is Martyn's extreme satire. More often than not the author overshoots the mark simply because he does not know how to sugar his pill. In *The Tale of a Town*, for instance, almost every Irishman cuts a poor figure and all the Englishmen are depicted as so many monsters. Where Ibsen mixes his scorn with sympathy and pity for humankind, as well as with subtle humour, the Irish dramatist is so blinded by his indignation that his satirical plays leave room for little else but the author's mockery and contempt.

Last but not least there are, of course, certain far-reaching differences between the two dramatists from the point of view of literary workmanship. After all it is only natural that Martyn's artistic limitations, such as faulty individualization and stilted dialogue, should become accentuated in the presence of the Norwegian giant.

---

[1] Although primarily a great poet and artist, Ibsen did raise his forefinger from time to time to point the moral of the play. Suffice it to mention *The Wild Duck*, generally considered to be his masterpiece.

But this is not the point. Many playwrights are dwarfed by Ibsen. The point is that the juxtaposition of Martyn's plays with those of his great forerunner reveals a remarkable correspondence of theme, character drawing, setting and technique. It is to the Irishman's credit that at least two of his plays compare favourably even with the finest works of Ibsen.

In an attempt to estimate the true significance of Edward Martyn's contribution to the Irish drama, one may say that his early plays are object lessons of what new conquests might be made within the world of the poetic drama thanks to the pioneering work of the Norwegian master-builder.

The Heather Field and some of the plays that were to follow no doubt formed a striking contrast to the uniform productions of the contemporary Irish stage. They showed the possibilities of a new kind of drama, a drama both Irish and cosmopolitan. Thus Martyn's plays, as well as the European repertory of his own theatre, set an example that paved the way for the continental drama.

"Edward Martyn and J. M. Synge," a contemporary critic writes, "have a very special claim to Ireland's gratitude and admiration. Without Edward Martyn, the modern Irish drama might never have been born. Without Synge, it would have died in early childhood. In congratulating the Abbey on its coming of age, let Irishmen pay tribute to the memory of Edward Martyn—a man of ideas, a man of courage, and a man who loved his people and his country well."[1]

---

[1] Quoted Denis Gwynn, *op. cit.*, p. 150.

Bibliography

Bibliography

A.

HENRIK IBSEN

1. PLAYS AND DRAFTS

Samlede Verker. Hundreårsutgave, ved Francis Bull, Halvdan Koht, Didrik Arup Seip. 21 vols. Gyldendal, Oslo 1928–1958.
Collected Works. Entirely revised and edited by William Archer. 12 vols. Heinemann, London 1906–1912.

Some of Ibsen's plays appeared almost simultaneously in Norway and in England. The majority of his prose dramas were accessible to the play-reading public in English, French, and German translations, published in the 1880's and 1890's. Ibsen's "dramatic epilogue" *When We Dead Awaken* (1899) was translated into English as early as 1900.

2. SPEECHES AND LETTERS

The Correspondence of Henrik Ibsen. Edited by Mary Morison. London 1905.

Speeches and New Letters. Translated and edited by Arne Kildal. With an introduction by Lee M. Hollander. Boston 1910.

This authorized edition of Ibsen's speeches and letters contains a very useful "chronological bibliography of Ibsen and the interest manifested in him in the English-speaking countries, as shown by translations, performances, and commentaries".

B.

EDWARD MARTYN

1. MANUSCRIPT PLAYS

The Privilege of Place[1]
The Path of Logic

----

[1] In a letter of December 8, 1959, Professor Stephen P. Ryan, who owns the unique MS., kindly informs the present writer that *The Privilege of Place*, *The Path of Logic* and *The Official's Son* are one and the same play. It was produced by Martyn's Irish Theatre in November, 1915, under the title *The Privilege of Place*.

The Official's Son
Gifford of Knockroe[1]
Regina Eyre[2]

2. PUBLISHED WORK

*Morgante the Lesser. His Notorious Life and Wonderful Deeds, arranged
and narrated for the first time by Sirius.* A satirical "novel". London 1890.

PLAYS

The Heather Field and *Maeve.* London 1899.
The Tale of a Town and *An Enchanted Sea.* London 1902.
The Place-Hunters. A political comedy in one act. Published in *The Leader*,
26 July, 1902.
Romulus and Remus or The Makers of Delights. A symbolist extravaganza
in one act. Published in the Christmas Supplement to William O'Brien's
Irish People, 21 December, 1907.
Grangecolman. Dublin 1912.
The Dream Physician. Dublin n.d.

SELECTED ESSAYS

"A Comparison between Irish and English Theatrical Audiences" in
Beltaine, February, 1900.
"The Palestrina Choir" in *The Leader*, 20 April, 1901.
"A Plea for a National Theatre in Ireland" in *Samhain*, 1901.
"Ireland's Battle for Her Language". *Gaelic League Pamphlets* No. 4.
"The Gaelic League and Irish Music" in *The Irish Review*, November,
1911.
"Wagner's Parsifal, or the Cult of Liturgical Aestheticism" in *The Irish
Review*, December, 1913.
"The Recent Performance of Ibsen's *Rosmersholm*" in *The Irish Review*,
February, 1914.
"A Plea for the Revival of the Irish Literary Theatre" in *The Irish
Review*, April, 1914.

---

[1] In the same letter Professor Ryan points out that "no mss of *Gifford of Knockroe* has turned up, and I presume it was lost with the other Martyn papers when
the Carmelite priory in London was destroyed by bombing in 1941". For an
abortive attempt to trace the missing papers, see Sister Marie-Thérèse Courtney,
Edward Martyn and the Irish Theatre (New York 1956), Preface and Appendix A.

[2] This play was Edward Martyn's last contribution to the Dublin stage. It was
performed by the Irish Theatre in April, 1919. (See Stephen P. Ryan, "Edward
Martyn's Last Play" in *Studies*, Summer 1958.)

C.

OTHER SOURCES

ANDREWS, CHARLTON. *The Drama To-day*. Philadelphia 1913.

ANTOINE, ANDRÉ. *"Mes Souvenirs" sur le Théâtre-Libre*. Paris 1921.

ARCHER, WILLIAM. "Introductions to Ibsen's Plays" in *Collected Works* (See A.)

—— (ed.) *From Ibsen's Workshop*. Notes, Scenarios, and Drafts of the Modern Plays. Vol. XII of *The Collected Works of Henrik Ibsen*. London 1912.

—— *The Old Drama and the New*. London 1923.

—— "Ibseniana" in *Edda*, XXXI (1931).

BARNES, T. R. "Yeats, Synge, Ibsen and Strindberg" in *Scrutiny* (ed. F. R. Leavis), V (1936).

BINSWANGER, LUDWIG. *Henrik Ibsen und das Problem der Selbstrealisation in der Kunst*. Heidelberg 1949.

BJERSBY (BRAMSBÄCK), BIRGIT. *The Interpretation of the Cuchulain Legend in the Works of W. B. Yeats*. Upsala Irish Studies I. Diss., Upsala 1950. (See also BRAMSBÄCK.)

BJØRNSON, BJØRNSTJERNE. *Plays: first series (The Gauntlet, Beyond Our Power, The New System)*, translated by Edwin Björkman. London 1913.

—— *Plays: second series (Love and Geography, Beyond Human Might, Laboremus)*, translated by Edwin Björkman. London 1913.

BOURGEOIS, MAURICE. *John Millington Synge and the Irish Theatre*. London 1913.

BOYD, ERNEST A. *Ireland's Literary Renaissance*. Dublin & London 1916.

—— *The Contemporary Drama of Ireland*. Boston 1917.

—— "The Abbey Theatre" in *The Irish Review*, February 1913.

BRADBROOK, M. C. *Ibsen the Norwegian. A Revaluation*. London 1946.

BRAMSBÄCK, BIRGIT. *James Stephens. A Literary and Bibliographical Study*. Upsala Irish Studies IV. Upsala & Lund 1959.

BRANDES, GEORG. *Henrik Ibsen* in *Die Literatur*, XXXII–XXXIII, Berlin n.d. With an extensive list of foreign translations of Ibsen's works up to 1906.

BRENEL, HJALMAR. *Etiska motiv i Henrik Ibsens dramatiska diktning*. Diss., Upsala 1941.

BROWN, MALCOLM. *George Moore. A Reconsideration*. Seattle 1955.

BROWN, STEPHEN J. (ed.) *A Guide to Books on Ireland*. Dublin 1912.

BULL, FRANCIS. *Ibsen. The Man and the Dramatist*. Oxford 1954.

—— *et alii*. *Norsk Litteraturhistorie*. 6 vols. Oslo 1924–1955.

BURCHARDT, C. B. *Norwegian Life and Literature*. London 1920.

BYRNE, DAWSON. *The Story of Ireland's National Theatre*. Dublin 1929.

CHANDLER, F. W. *Aspects of Modern Drama*. New York 1914.
—— *Modern Continental Playwrights*. New York & London 1931.
CLARK, BARRETT H. *A Study of the Modern Drama*. New York & London 1936.
CLARK, B. H. and FREEDLEY, G. *A History of Modern Drama*. Edited by Clark and Freedley. New York & London 1947.
CLARK, JAMES M. "The Irish Literary Movement" in *Englische Studien*, XLIX (1915–1916).
COLUM, MARY. *Life and the Dream*. New York 1947.
COLUM, PADRAIC. *Arthur Griffith*. Dublin 1959.
CORKERY, DANIEL. *Synge and Anglo-Irish Literature*. Oxford 1931, 1947.
COURTNEY, SISTER MARIE-THÉRÈSE. *Edward Martyn and the Irish Theatre*. Diss., New York 1956.
CUMMINS, GERALDINE. *Dr. E. Œ. Somerville. A Biography*. London 1952.
CUNLIFFE, J. W. *English Literature during the Last Half-Century*. London 1923.
—— *Modern English Playwrights*. New York 1927.

DECKER, CLARENCE R. "Ibsen in England" in *The American Scandinavian Review*, XLI (Summer 1953).
DIKKA REQUE, A. *Trois auteurs dramatiques scandinaves. Ibsen, Björnson, Strindberg devant la critique française 1889–1901*. Diss., Paris 1930.
DOWNS, BRIAN W. *Ibsen. The Intellectual Background*. Cambridge 1946.
—— *A Study of Six Plays by Ibsen*. Cambridge 1950.
—— "Anglo-Norwegian Literary Relations 1867–1900" in *Modern Language Review*. XLVII (1952.)
DUGGAN, G. C. *The Stage Irishman. A History of the Irish Play and Stage Character from the Earliest Times*. London & New York 1937.
DUVE, ARNE. *Symbolikken i Henrik Ibsens skuespill*. Oslo 1945.

EGLINTON, JOHN *et alii. Literary Ideals in Ireland*. London 1899.
—— *Anglo-Irish Essays*. Dublin 1917.
—— *Irish Literary Portraits*. London 1935.
ELLIS-FERMOR, UNA. *The Irish Dramatic Movement*. London 1939, 1954.
—— Introduction to *Three Plays* by Ibsen. ("The Penguin Classics") London 1950.
ELLMAN, RICHARD. *Yeats: The Man and the Masks*. London 1949.

FARINELLI, ARTURO. *Führende Geister des Nordens. Geist und Poesi der Skandinavier Björnson, Strindberg, Ibsen*. Stuttgart 1940.
FAY, GERARD. *The Abbey Theatre*. London 1958.
FEHR, BERNHARD. *Die englische Literatur des 19. und 20. Jahrhunderts*. Berlin 1923.
FERGUSSON, FRANCIS. *The Idea of a Theater*. New York 1949.

FILON, A. "Ibsen à Londres—le drame de demain" in *La Revue des deux mondes*, CXXXII (1895).

FRAENKL, PAVEL. *Ibsens vei til drama. En undersøkelse av dramatikerens genesis.* Oslo 1955.

FRANC, MIRIAM. *Ibsen in England.* Diss., Boston, Mass. 1919.

FRASER, G. S. *The Modern Writer and His World.* London 1953.

FREEMAN, JOHN. *A Portrait of George Moore in a Study of His Work.* London 1922.

GOSSE, EDMUND. *Ibsen.* ("Literary Lives Series") London 1907.

GRAN, GERHARD. *Henrik Ibsen. Liv og verker.* 2 vols. Kristiania 1918.

GREENE, DAVID H. and STEPHENS, EDWARD M. *J. M. Synge 1871–1909.* New York 1959.

GREGORY, LADY AUGUSTA. *Our Irish Theatre.* London & New York 1913.

—— *Visions and Beliefs in the West of Ireland.* London 1920.

—— *Journals 1916–1930.* Edited by Lennox Robinson. Dublin 1946.

GUYARD, M.-F. *La littérature comparée.* Paris 1951.

GWYNN, DENIS. *Edward Martyn and the Irish Revival.* London 1930.

GWYNN, STEPHEN. *Irish Literature and Drama.* London 1936.

HENN, T. R. *The Lonely Tower. Studies in the Poetry of W. B. Yeats.* London 1950.

HOGAN, J. J. *W. B. Yeats.* Dublin 1939.

HOLLOWAY, JOSEPH. *Impressions of a Dublin Playgoer.* National Library of Ireland MS.

—— "Some Books about the Theatre in Ireland" and "Irish Plays" in *A Guide to Books on Ireland* (ed. S. J. Brown). Dublin 1912.

HONE, JOSEPH. *The life of George Moore.* London 1936.

—— *W. B. Yeats 1865–1939.* London 1942.

HOPPER, VINCENT F. and GREBANIER, BERNARD. *Essentials of European Literature.* 2 vols. ("Barron's Educational Series") Brooklyn, N.Y., 1953.

HOWARTH, HERBERT. *The Irish Writers 1880–1940.* London 1958.

HUBER, ROBERT. *Ibsens Bedeutung für das englische Drama.* Diss., Marburg/L. 1914.

HYDE, DOUGLAS. *A Literary History of Ireland.* London 1899.

HAAKONSEN, DANIEL. *Henrik Ibsens realisme.* Oslo 1957.

HØST, ELSE. *Hedda Gabler. En monografi.* Diss., Oslo 1958.

IBSEN, BERGLIOT. *De tre. Erindringer om Henrik Ibsen, Suzannah Ibsen, Sigurd Ibsen.* Oslo 1948.

—— (*The Three Ibsens.* New York 1952).

IBSEN-ÅRBOK I–V. Utgiven ved Einar Østvedt. Skien 1952–1959.

JACKSON, HOLBROOK. *The Eighteen Nineties. A Review of Art and Ideas at the Close of the Nineteenth Century.* London 1913.

JACOBS, MONTY. *Ibsens Bühnentechnik*. Dresden 1920.
JEFFARES, NORMAN A. *W.B. Yeats. Man and Poet*. London 1949.
JEPSON, EDGAR. "The Norse Renascence" in *To-Morrow*, III (1897).

KAVANAGH, PETER. *The Irish Theatre*. Tralee 1946.
KEHLER, HENNING. "Studier i det ibsenske Drama" in *Edda*, IV–V (1915–1916).
KOHT, HALVDAN. *Henrik Ibsen. Eit diktarliv*. Ny, omarbeidd utgåve. 2 vols. Oslo 1954.
KRÖNER, JOHANNA. *Die Technik des realistischen Dramas bei Ibsen und Galsworthy*. Diss., Munich. Published in *Beiträge zur englischen Philologie*, XXVIII, Leipzig 1935.

LAMM, MARTIN. "Ibsen och Tjekov" in *Edda* XLVII (1947).
—— *Det moderna dramat*. Stockholm 1948.
—— *Modern Drama*. Translated by Karin Elliott. Oxford 1952.
LAVRIN, JANKO. *Ibsen and His Creation*. London 1921.
—— *Studies in European Literature*. London 1929.
—— *Ibsen. An Approach*. London 1950.
LAW, HUGH. *Anglo-Irish Literature*. Dublin & London 1926.
LEE, JENNETTE. *The Ibsen Secret. A Key to the Prose Dramas of Henrik Ibsen*. New York & London 1907.
LEGOUIS, EMILE and CAZAMIAN, LOUIS. *A History of English Literature*. London 1943.
LESCOFFIER, J. *Histoire de la littérature norvégienne*. Paris 1952.
DE LIPSKI, W. "Note sur le Symbolisme de W. B. Yeats" in *Etudes anglaises*, IV (1940).

MCFARLANE, JAMES WALTER. *Ibsen and the Temper of Norwegian Literature* London 1960.
MAC LIAMMÓIR, MICHEÁL. "Problem Plays" in *The Irish Theatre*, ed. by Lennox Robinson. London 1939.
—— *Theatre in Ireland*. Dublin 1950.
MACNAMARA, BRINSLEY (ed.) *Abbey Plays 1899–1948*. Dublin n.d.
MAETERLINCK, MAURICE. *Théâtre*. 3 vols. Brussels & Paris 1901–1902.
MAIR, G. H. *English Literature: Modern*. London 1914.
MALONE, ANDREW E. *The Irish Drama*. London 1929.
MARCEL, GABRIEL and de LACRETELLE, JACQUES. "Hommage à Ibsen" in *Revue d'Histoire du Théâtre*, IX (1957).
MITCHELL, SUSAN L. *George Moore*. Dublin & London 1916.
MOORE, GEORGE. *The Bending of the Bough*. London 1900.
—— *'Hail and Farewell!' A Trilogy. Ave* (1911); *Salve* (1912); *Vale* (1914). London 1947.
MORGAN, A. E. *Tendencies of Modern English Drama*. London 1924.
MORGAN, CHARLES. *Epitaph on George Moore*. London 1935.
MOSFJELD, OSKAR. *Henrik Ibsen og Skien*. Diss., Oslo 1949.

NEJDEFORS-FRISK, SONJA. *George Moore's Naturalistic Prose. Upsala Irish Studies* III. Lund 1952.

NICOLL, ALLARDYCE. *The English Theatre.* London 1936.

—— *British Drama.* London 1947.

—— *The Development of the Theatre.* London 1949.

—— *A History of Late Nineteenth Century Drama 1850–1900.* 2 vols. Cambridge 1949.

—— *World Drama.* London & Sidney 1949, 1951.

NILSSON, NILS ÅKE. *Ibsen in Russland. Etudes de philologie slave* VII. Stockholm 1958.

NISSEN, INGJALD. *Sjelelige kriser i menneskets liv. Henrik Ibsen og den moderne psykologi.* Oslo 1931.

NORTHAM, JOHN. *Ibsen's Dramatic Method. A Study of the Prose Dramas.* London 1953.

O'HANLON, HENRY B. *The All-Alone.* With a preface by Edward Martyn. Dublin 1919.

PEACOCK, RONALD. *The Art of Drama.* New York 1956.

POGSON, REX. *Miss Horniman and the Gaiety Theatre, Manchester.* London 1952.

PRAZ, MARIO. *The Romantic Agony.* London 1933.

QVAMME, BØRRE. "Ibsen og det engelske teater" in *Edda*, XLII (1942).

REYNOLDS, ERNEST. *Modern English Drama. A Survey of the Theatre from 1900.* London 1949.

RIVOALLAN, A. *Littérature irlandaise contemporaine.* Paris 1939.

ROBINSON, LENNOX (ed.) *The Irish Theatre.* Lectures delivered during the Abbey Theatre Festival in Dublin in August 1938. London 1939.

—— (ed.) *Lady Gregory's Journals 1916–1930.* Dublin 1946.

RUBOW, P. V. *Two Essays: Henrik Ibsen—The Sagas.* Copenhagen 1949.

RYAN, STEPHEN P. "Edward Martyn's Last Play" in *Studies*, XLVII (1958).

RYDELL, GERDA. *Henrik Ibsen. En orientering i hans liv och diktning.* Stockholm 1932.

SCOTT-JAMES, R. A. *Fifty Years of English Literature. 1900–1950.* London 1951.

SETTERQUIST, JAN. *Ibsen and the Beginnings of Anglo-Irish Drama.* I. *John Millington Synge. Upsala Irish Studies* II. Upsala 1951.

—— "Ibsen på Den gröna ön" in *Ord och bild*, LXII (1953).

—— "Ibsen and Edward Martyn" *Edda* (To be published in 1960.)

SHAW, BERNARD. *The Quintessence of Ibsenism. Now Completed to the Death of Ibsen.* London 1913.
—— *Plays and Players.* Essays on the Theatre. Selected with an Introduction by A. C. Ward. ("The World's Classics") London 1955.
STRINDBERG, AUGUST. *Eight Famous Plays: The Father; Miss Julia; The Stronger; The Link; There Are Crimes and Crimes; Gustavus Vasa; The Dance of Death; The Spook Sonata.* Translated by Edwin Björkman and N. Erichsen. With an Introduction by Alan Harris. London 1949.
STUYVER, CLARA. *Ibsens dramatische Gestalten. Psychologie und Symbolik.* Amsterdam 1952.
SYMONS, ARTHUR. *The Symbolist Movement in Literature.* London 1899.
—— *Studies in Prose and Verse.* London 1904.
—— *Dramatis Personae.* London 1925.

TENNANT, P. F. D. *Ibsen's Dramatic Technique.* Cambridge 1948.
TIEGHEM, PAUL VAN. *La littérature comparée.* Paris 1931.

UNTERECKER, JOHN. *A Reader's Guide to William Butler Yeats.* London 1959.
WADE, ALLAN. *A Bibliography of the Writings of W. B. Yeats.* London 1951.
WEIGAND, HERMAN J. *The Modern Ibsen. A Reconsideration.* New York 1925.
WEYGANDT, CORNELIUS. *Irish Plays and Playwrights.* London 1913.
WILLIAMS, HAROLD. *Modern English Writers.* London 1918.
WILLIAMS, RAYMOND. *Drama from Ibsen to Eliot.* London 1952.
WILSON, F. A. C. *W. B. Yeats and Tradition.* New York 1958.

YEATS, W. B. "The Literary Movement in Ireland" in *North American Review,* CLXIX (1899).
—— "Maive and Certain Irish Beliefs" in *Beltaine,* 1900.
—— *Plays and Controversies.* London 1923.
—— *Essays (1896–1917).* London 1924.
—— *The Bounty of Sweden: A Meditation, and a Lecture delivered before the Royal Swedish Academy and Certain Notes by William Butler Yeats.* Dublin 1925.
—— *Dramatis Personae.* London 1936.
—— *Essays (1931–1936).* Dublin 1937.
—— *Collected Plays.* London 1952.
—— (ed.) *Beltaine.* An Occasional Publication. I–III. May 1899–April 1900. London & Dublin.
—— (The three numbers of *Beltaine* were also published in a separate volume. London n.d.)
—— (ed.) *Samhain.* An Occasional Review. I–VII. October 1901–November 1908. London & Dublin.

Index*

Index*

* The Roman numerals I and II refer to vols. I and II of the present investigation.

WITHDRAWN